THE JOURNEY of LIFE & PURPOSE with GOD

C. M. FARRELL

First published in 2021 by Pere Publishing Ltd

ISBN 978-1-5262-0874-3

Copyright © Charlotte Farrell 2021

The right of Charlotte Farrell to be identified as the author of this work has been asserted by her in accordance with the Copyright, Designs and Patents Act 1998.

All rights reserved. No part of this publication may be reproduced, stored in a retrieval system, or transmitted in any form, or by any means (electronic, mechanical, photocopying, recording or otherwise) without the prior written permission of the publisher, nor be otherwise circulated in any form of binding or cover other than that in which it is published and without a similar condition including this condition being imposed on the subsequent purchaser.

Neither the publisher nor the author is engaged in rendering professional advice or services to the individual reader. The ideas, procedures, and suggestions contained in this book are not intended as a substitute for consulting with a suitable professional i.e Priest, Pastor, Counsellor, Therapist.

Pere Publishing Ltd does not have any control over, or any responsibility for any author or third-party websites referred to in or on this book.

Cover and interior design by KUHN Design Group | kuhndesigngroup.com

Printed and bound in USA by IngramSpark

ACKNOWLEDGEMENTS

My profound thanks and gratitude to God for every revelation, His grace and faithfulness in life and making this book come to be.

Thanks to my family & friends for your love and encouragement, and to every person who has challenged me along my life journey; Every experience has brought me to this point.

Thanks to my love Daniel, you are my greatest motivation to become all that God has destined me to be. I love you and I pray you constantly step into, inhabit, fulfil and enjoy all that God has prepared for you.

CONTENTS

Introduction 7

1. The Word 11
2. Relationship Building 15
3. The Power of God's Word 21
4. Surrender 35
5. Growing Pains 43
6. Failure 55
7. Success Is… 63
8. The Changes We Go Through 73
9. New Identity New Power 81
10. Trials, Tests & Temptations 93
11. The Growth Process 107
12. Living Your Destiny 117
13. Your Calling & Purpose 125
14. Salutation 129

INTRODUCTION

"There are three monumental landmark moments in life; The day you were born, the day you discover why you were born, and the day you begin to walk in your purpose".

L ife is one of the most precious gifts that we will ever be blessed with, and as quoted above, knowing the purpose for which we have been created is critical. God has created, designed and fashioned each of our lives in such a way that when we fulfil the 'why' we achieve greatness and impact the world in a way that only we can. It is however a sad reality that most people travel through life following the same daily routines totally unaware that there is a hidden destiny that awaits us if we dare to travel it. It's a daring journey of venturing into the unknown and few actually dare to leave the comfort and security of their predictable lives to step out and discover it. From our youths we're conditioned to believe a narrative of what life should look like; go to school, college and university, get a job, establish a successful career, do good works, marry, have kids and raise them, fit in your hobbies in between time and then gracefully age, retire and pass away. More often than not we go through life measuring the hallmarks of our success based upon how we excel in these things, or even how much wealth we accumulate in comparison to people. But we seriously need to ask ourselves whether this is really the purpose for our lives. Was it God's intention to create our lives for the purpose of us to methodically go through countless routines all the days of our lives, accumulate stuff and accolades? I suggest not! Each of our lives have been strategically designed in the mind of God with a specific purpose, plan and path. They are an intentional act of God's will, and the single greatest achievement that we can ever make on this earth is to discover and fulfil the plan and purpose for our lives.

Discovering our purpose is no mean feat and we begin this journey of discovery by developing the practice of stillness, which involves tuning out from the busyness of this world. We need that space, calm and solitude for introspection—the study of our innermost thoughts and being, and how it relates to God, His Word and how all of that leads us into our destiny. It is the most amazing lifelong journey that we could ever experience if we dare to step out in faith one step at a time.

Whilst this book dare not hold itself out as having the answers to life's existential questions, what it does is help you explore and identify areas in your life that may require change and alignment to best position you to grow into your purpose to live a fulfilling and happy life. This book also helps you to explore how the bible can be used as a tool to help and empower you to develop your relationship with God and discover the purpose for which you've been created. As you go through this book, feel free to make notes in the notes section at the back, so you can capture thoughts as they come to you.

By the end of this book, you will have a more enriched understanding of the purpose of God's Word and understand strategies of how to apply it to your life in order to develop your relationship with God. This will bring clarity to the significance of God and His Word in our everyday lives and will guide you onto a life-changing journey of fulfillment and purpose.

• • •

CHAPTER ONE

THE WORD

*'In the beginning was the Word, and the Word
was with God, and the Word was God.'*

JOHN 1:1

THE IMPORTANCE OF WORDS

We often take for granted how important words are as a communication tool. In their simplest form they convey our thoughts and intentions to each other in life. Without words we would simply be lost in understanding and communicating with the world around us, and as such they form an integral part of our understanding and relationship with the world. This is why it is such a huge milestone when a child begins to speak. Up to that point there are limitations on the depths of our communication. We often see parents and caregivers spend endless amounts of time speaking to children, reading to them and teaching them about the world around them. Words are used to educate them about the purpose of different toys, boundaries and danger. However when a child begins to speak it opens up a whole new world of communication and relationship building because the child can now communicate its needs and desires far more effectively and closer relationships are formed.

In the simplest of terms, words are effectively invisible packages that transport intentions, wills, desires and information. Words are critical to the efficient functioning of life. If this is how integral words are in being able to teach a child about the world that they have just come into, then how much more critical are words when we are trying to grow and understand the Words of God Our Father. Since our souls' original home is in the spirit realm of eternity with God, He has given us His Word to grow the core part of our being, our spirit, and to help us navigate our destined life path in this new realm. God's Word is the bible and He has given it to us to convey His intentions, thoughts, plans and purposes for which He created for our lives. His Word is also there to help us maintain our relationship and connection with Him much like children use words to communicate and bond with their parents. His Word is the torch and the tool that directs us in successfully fulfilling the purposes that our lives were created for. If we dare to step out and diligently apply His Word to our lives it will most certainly lead us into the mind-blowing destiny that awaits us.

THE SPIRIT REALM

The spirit realm is not something that many of us give a second thought to in our day-to-day living. It's an unseen realm and let's be honest unless we've had certain experiences we may never even really acknowledge that it exists. Whether we choose to acknowledge it or not the fact remains that the spirit realm is a very real life form that exists beyond what we can see and is the parallel universe from where our soul originates. Unless we are attuned to it we may not even have any experience of it, although I'm not talking about any of that hocus pocus stuff (although witchcraft does also involve the spirit realm but is not within the remit of this book). The point here is that life did not suddenly begin the moment we were birthed into this physical world. Only life '*as we know it*' begins at birth but in reality we were souls that existed in the spirit realm way before the conception process! The physical formation of cells, organs and the like is only the beginning of the physical manifestations of life in this physical realm. The cells form our bodies, and when combined with our souls and the life giving spirit of God within us, we then experience life as we know it. It is the spirit of God that causes our souls and bodies to partake in this experience of life on earth because God is a Spirit and the Source of all life (Numbers 27:16).

Before we entered the encasement of our human bodies, and even before our bodies began to form in our mother's womb we were *first* souls that existed in relationship with God in the spirit realm. He knew us from that long ago, way before we were formed in our mother's womb and even before the foundations of the earth were laid. From since our soul's existence in eternity with God, He assigned a purpose to each of us that we have been destined to complete on earth at a particular time in world's existence. That is how our lives were decided and our birth determined. Our parents are the vessels God used to bring us into and this physical world, and when all these elements came together as God intended it we arrived on earth experiencing life as we know it.

> "*Before I formed you in the womb I knew you, before you were born I set you apart; I appointed you as a prophet to the nations.*" —Jeremiah 1:5

Our lives are absolutely no mistake whatsoever. The circumstances of our birth may not have been planned, intended or even wanted by our parents however that does not negate the fact that in the mind of God, He deliberately created us for a purpose. Whilst we are here on earth it is our primary job to reconnect with God, re-establish our relationship with Him and allow God to reveal and lead us into our life's purpose. It is only when we reconnect with Him and living the lives we were intended to live that we can feel intrinsically fulfilled.

As we know there are many people seeking fulfilment in all manner of things from jobs and relationships to material wealth. When all that fails to fill the void sadly people turn to things like drugs and alcohol. At our very core we have been created with a void which is the cause of our sense of longing and fulfilment. That void has been designed only to be properly filled by God, and when that happens we begin to experience true fulfilment within our lives. It is only at the point when re-establish our relationship with God and walk with Him that we become on track to walking in the daily fulfilment of our life's purpose. Many people before us have tried and failed to fill that void with other things; The truth is that nothing and no-one else but God has the capacity to provide the fulfilment of the void, but when we begin to live in relationship with Him and fulfilment of our purpose that void begins to fill and we experience that sense of fulfilment for which many have been seeking.

• • •

CHAPTER TWO

RELATIONSHIP BUILDING

"Draw near to God and He will draw near to you"

JAMES 4:8

DEVELOPING A RELATIONSHIP WITH GOD

Just like any successful relationship it is essential to have communication both ways. Our relationship with God is no different. If we're going to be real, let's admit that there have been times where we've only gone to God in a moment of desperation and not genuinely seeking to communicate to build our relationship. As we know that is a selfish way to try and build any relationship! Imagine how unpleasant it would feel being in a relationship with someone knowing that they only sought us out when they wanted something. In fact I'm sure many of us know people like that and the likelihood is that those are not the best quality relationships in our lives. The same applies to God. If we want to re-establish our relationship with Him then we need to create more regular and consistent communication with Him. In doing so we understand more about His carefully designed intentional plans for our lives and begin to fulfil them. It can be hard to fully grasp this, but whilst we're busy getting on with our lives how we think best, God is there patiently waiting for us to communicate with Him whilst He holds in His hand the plans, destiny and future that He created for our lives. Unfortunately we can be so busy with our own minds that many times people live their whole lives without ever spending that time with God, seeking Him and discovering the full potential of their lives.

Think about how excited a new parents are. For many months they have waited patiently for the baby to be born and baby finally arrives the parents are beyond excited. They literally cannot get enough of their new-born. I imagine it is like this and far beyond for God. He has known our souls and the plans He has created for our lives for way longer than our parents. Part of the transition from the spirit realm into this physical realm of earth means that we lose our knowledge of God; Our human conscious minds do not have the capacity to remember our experience or relationship with God. That is a significant loss to God who has invested so much in us, and therefore He longs to reconnect His relationship with us so that we can walk in the awesome fulfilment of the plans and destiny that He has carefully created for our lives.

Having this insight makes it all the more dismal for us when we understand how selfish we have been when we've only sought God when we wanted something from Him, if we even ever acknowledged Him at all before now. Therefore in life if we want to know our true identity and the purpose for which we have been created, we need to stop seeking God for 'things' or hasty answers to our prayers, and begin to develop a deep and meaningful relationship with Him during our time on earth so that we can reconnect with Him and fulfil the life plans that He created us for. When we understand this it becomes clearer that the point of life is to fulfil our God-given purpose. It's not a phrase that we should loosely throw around, but it is at the very core of our being, the reason why we have the void to seek Him out, and is reason why we're here on earth. Living daily in relationship with God brings us closer to filling the void in our lives and into the fulfilment of our life's purpose providing a sense of true and intrinsic joy, and in time success.

LIFE CHOICES

Everything here on earth is temporary, including our own physical existence of life on earth. Eventually our souls return to the spirit realm and our bodies return into the earth. As such we are faced with the decision of how we are going to life the lives that we have been given. Do we wish to use it to fulfil our God-given purpose and the reason we've been created, or will we choose to pursue life according to our own wishes and desires. The choice is entirely ours, and God has admonished us in His Word (the bible) to choose wisely.

> *Now what I am commanding you today is not too difficult for you or beyond your reach.... The word is very near you... so you may obey it. See I set before you today life and prosperity, death and destruction. For I command you today to love the Lord your God, to walk in obedience to him and to keep his commands... then you will live and increase, and the Lord your God will bless you.* —Deuteronomy 30: 11-15

HOW TO DEVELOP OUR RELATIONSHIP WITH GOD

As seen in the earlier example, children develop their relationship with their parents when they begin to be able to communicate with them using Words. The same applies for our relationship with God. In order to reconnect with Him we have to spend time reading and understanding His Word (the bible). Just like children learn about their parents' characters from their words and behaviours, so too do we learn about God and His character by understanding His Words and His ways that are laid out in countless examples throughout the bible. It is literally full of accounts where people have experienced the phenomenal presence and involvement of God within their everyday lives. He has given us these examples of how He helped people in the past to live their lives to guide us and empower us with confidence that not only can we trust Him, but that we can also *depend* on Him to help us fulfil the plans and purposes that He has created for us to fulfil. It is also worth noting that the bible is also full of examples of people who decided to reject God by not trusting Him. They decided not to live life according to His word, but do their own thing. Although they may have had some success for a time, in the end it wasn't at all worth it because that success didn't last and they paid for it with their souls, having to spend eternity without God.

WE ARE GOD'S MASTERPIECE– HE'S OUR BIGGEST INVESTOR

Consider this allegorical example. Think of God as a wealthy investor who invested $100 trillion dollars into a particular project. Any such an investor takes great care to monitor with acute interest how the project is progressing, what factors are affecting it, and how he may exert influence over the environment of his investment in order to protect it. All of these measures are taken to ensure that the investment accomplishes its purpose—to make a profit. In much the same way God invested a great destiny within us when He created us. He is keenly interested to be involved in every detail in our lives because He knows our destiny and what we need in order to get to the next level. The way that parents of a newborn keenly await the birth of their baby, and are attentive to its every need upon arrival, this mirrors God's attentiveness and joy when our souls enter this earth realm. His eyes are upon us as He patiently waits for us to decide to reconnect with Him so that He can guide us into the destiny that He has prepared for us to fulfill on earth. In fact, when we commit our lives and our ways to God, He puts a hedge of protection around us to help us live according to our destiny and stop the enemy from ruining our lives, just like He did for Job (Job 1:10).

And don't think that because we're on a highly populated earth that somehow God will forget about us or our destiny. Definitely not, God knows everything, He is omniscient and it is impossible for Him to forget about us! In fact He is so invested in us and our destiny that He has given us His Word that He will never ever leave us nor forsake us. Not just, that but God made the ultimate sacrifice for our souls. God made His Word become human flesh in the form of Jesus Christ, and God sacrificed His Word, His only Son. He did this so that by accepting His Word as our supreme guide and authority for life, we would be reconnected back into relationship with Him. When we decide that the mission of our lives is to live according to God's Word, Jesus becomes our Lord. When we decide to accept that Jesus paid the price of our sins so that we could be reconnected back into relationship with God, Jesus becomes our Saviour.

A SPECIAL GIFT

In addition to paying the ultimate price to restore us back into relationship with Him, God has also given us His power to live within us as a guide to direct us through life. This power is called the Holy Spirit, and we receive it when we accept God's Word (Jesus Christ) as the ultimate power and authority in our lives. The Holy Spirit is a person and is quite literally God's Holy Spirit, and God's divine mechanism to guide us, give us peace, strength and power to deal with the full range of life's challenging situations. The Holy Spirit gives us wisdom to know the right thing to do in our lives and to be able to distinguish between things that are from God, and counterfeits that pretend to be from God that come to take us of our predestined path. It is by the Holy Spirit's power that we manage to live our lives in an acceptable way to God and the power by which we fulfil our destiny.

Knowing that God's Holy Spirit lives within our physical bodies makes our bodies a very place, something akin to a temple or church. We have to maintain that level of holiness in order to live with a steady stream of God's power in our lives and ability to receive His guidance to navigate our decision-making. When we live our lives in submission to God's Word and by the power of His Holy Spirit, we are walking in the most powerful state that we possibly could, and are on perfect course to fulfilling our destiny. Conversely when we don't obey God's Word and ignore the small still voice of the Holy Spirit gently guiding us, we curtail our capacity to fulfil our God-given destiny by minimising His power and authority in our lives. It is the difference between truly living in purpose, and passing the days of our life according to our own futile knowledge and understanding.

...

CHAPTER THREE

THE POWER OF GOD'S WORD

EVERYTHING WE NEED

We've often heard it said that a man is as good as his word, and with God this is an absolute truth because God IS His Word (John 1:1). Unlike a novel that contains a collection of empty words, God's Word actually carries power; The power of His Holy Spirit! This is the same power that God used to create the universe, and is the very essence of God. As such when we speak God's Word we are speaking the power and force of God into and over our lives. Every single word of God is full of His spirit and life (John 6:63). God's Word is purposeful and multi-dimensional because it has power both on earth and in the spirit realm. When we live our lives in submission to the authority of God's Word, we actually surrender the power of our life to the authority of God. If you can imagine it, our lives are like the vehicle that God uses to fulfil the plans that He created for us. The fuel that enables the vehicle to move and perform is His Word is the Holy Spirit. When we put His Word into our vehicle (hearts) and move forward (walking in faith) we can be sure that we have the power to travel and fulfil every single plan, path and purpose that God has predestined for us. Now that is some assurance!

HOW GOD'S WORD WORKS

We know by the Genesis account of the Bible that God actually created the entire universe by His Word. As He spoke it, the Spirit of God within His Word performed exactly what God said. God said *"light be"* and then there was light (Genesis 1:3).

As God created us in His image, we create and fulfil our purpose in the same manner of speaking God's Word. As discussed earlier, when we enter a committed relationship with God He gives us His Holy Spirit to live within us, which is the actual power of God within us. The way that we activate the Holy Spirit's power in our lives is by living out and speaking aloud God's Word over and through our life situations. Effectively this is prayer—submitting our lives and our will under the power of God's Word, and speaking its power over and into our life situations. How do we know if we have sin in our heart? How do we know if we're doing the right thing? We go into our quiet place where it's just us and God and we search His Word, find the principle of truth that aligns with our situation, and then we speak to God about it. Tell Him where we're at, there's no point in hiding it since God already knows every moment of our life from beginning to end. This dialogue with God is less about telling Him where we are, as it is about us confessing from our soul where we are, where we've missed it this time, and asking God to forgive us and help us to do things the way that He has destined in His Word. This practical application of God's Word to our life is what brings forth power, purpose and ultimately fulfilment. Life is busy and full of distractions so in order to be intentional about living out God's Word and will for our lives, we have to be intentional and conscious about developing the habit of regularly speaking to God throughout our day. This can be in a specific place that we have set aside, or it can be as spontaneous as when we commute through our daily lives. It matters not so much about the logistics of doing it, but more about actually routinely incorporating it as a regular habit in our lives. The important and fundamental thing is to ensure that we are intentional and regular about seeking out God's Word and checking out whether our desires and plans align with the principles of His Word.

We need to remember this, God knows exactly what we are facing in every facet of our life situations. By approaching God and His Word for guidance we are acknowledging that He is God in our lives, and that we accept that He has all knowledge and wisdom whatever we are facing. That kind of humility and submission pleases God, and He is absolutely faithful to guide us along the right path for our lives. When the bible says that we should pray at all times, it is because God is always there every single step of the way as we walk along our life path. If we just take the time to acknowledge His presence, power and wisdom we will routine experience His power and presence in our lives leading us into right paths and decisions that are good for our lives.

> *The Lord is my Shepherd.. He leads me along right paths.*
> *I will fear no evil for you are with me....* —Psalm 23

This regular communication that we initiate with God is in fact prayer. It is the mechanism through which we release God's power and presence into our lives and how we intimately involve Him to guide us to fulfil our destined purpose, each step, each moment through good habits and decisions each day.

The key to being able to trust God more and more with our life decisions is by becoming more familiar with the principles of His Word. The more we do this, the more we know Him and trust Him with our life situations to guide us into good decision-making that aligns with His will.

Sometimes this will not be easy, but the more we persevere through life's difficulties trusting God's Word to guide us, even in our most desperate situations that is the place where our faith truly grows and develops. Ultimately the more we demonstrate our faith to God, the more He will begin to reveal to us visions of the destiny that He has planned for our lives. Often times when we look back over our lives we can connect the dots to where God has aligned each and every situation, good, painful and indifferent to bring us to this very moment that we're in. Knowing that unbeknown to us God has masterfully orchestrated so many of life's moments in perfect symphony to work out our path to this point gives us assurance that He is faithful to continue to guide us, even when we cannot see the way for ourselves. Sometimes that guidance is revealed in dreams or visions. Often time it looks like an absolute impossibility, and this is quite typically a hallmark of God. He specialises in impossible situations, which are designed to stretch our faith and trust in Him as He leads us to fulfil an extraordinary and fulfilling destiny for our lives.

PRACTICALLY APPLYING THE WORD TO OUR LIVES

It all sounds perfectly logical however when we are in the midst of life's sometimes very tricky and testing situations, what we need in that exact moment is God's wisdom to know how to apply the principles of His Word to resolve our situations. So how do we go about doing this? This chapter is about exploring just that, but let's be very clear—there are no shortcuts or quick fixes to walking out God's Word in our lives. It takes time to learn His word, understand it and acquire the wisdom to know what to do, but we get there by each day regularly developing and nurturing our relationship with God.

In the small moments, in the big moment and in the everyday ordinary moments, it's about developing the habit of searching out God's principles in His word to guide our lives, developing our relationship with Him through talking things over with Him in prayer and essentially developing our relationship with Him. The more consistently and consciously we do this, the more we will recognise His undeniable presence in our lives. I often refer to these as 'God Friended Me' moments. The more conscious we become about seeking out God in our lives the more God Friended Me moments we will see. That in itself ignites a passion and curiosity to learn more about Him through His Word. As we do this God gives us understanding and wisdom for our life situations. It comes step by step, day by day and moment by moment. There is no great big 'ta-da' moment. It is in the small and faithful moments of developing our relationship with Him through His word and regular communication that we grow into the fulfilment of our destined being and fulfilment of our life's purpose.

Ultimately, this process we go through of living with a God-consciousness is all about reconfiguring our minds, and how we perceive life and its situations. Contrary to the world's culture of doing things, God's way for life doesn't require us to figure it all out. God already has it all figured out!

> *"Before I formed you in the womb I knew you, and before you were born I set you apart and appointed you as a prophet to the nations."* —Jeremiah 1:5

We would save ourselves a lot of stress and heartache if we were to just change our mindsets from trying to figure it all out ourselves and instead seek God's direction for our lives first.

God's Word actually tells us that if we seek His way first, which is the right way, all the things we want *[to be or achieve]* will be given to us if we follow the path that God is leading us along (Matthew 6:33).

God put passions and ambitions within our hearts to achieve certain things in accordance with the destiny that He prepared for us, even before we were born. But it is this worldly culture that makes us believe that we have to be Go-Getters and make things happen all for ourselves. That's not entirely true. We are to go get God's direction and then put our faith into action by pursuing the Word of direction that He has given us. We are not meant to be walking blindly trying to figure it all out for ourselves making endless mistakes, repeating bad cycles and experiencing pain. God knows the right way, He has prepared the paths to lead us to where we fulfil our desires and purpose. God calls them paths of righteousness, and it's our job to seek Him, know Him and get about following the path that He directs us along.

A NEW PERCEPTION OF LIFE: CHANGE

A critical step in travelling the journey of our destiny is linked to our willingness to change. It's not just about changing our behaviours, but also changing the way we process our thoughts and make decisions. This is often the most challenging part. We know that we need God's guidance on how to navigate the situations of our lives but if we're being real, that often seem so 'other worldly' when we're in the midst of a situation and we need a right-now kind of answer! However we have a right-now kind of God but we don't always think of Him in this way.

Consider this analogy; Imagine that we're taking a long-distance course by Skype. We need to complete the course to qualify for our dream job. In this analogy God is the Course Leader. He is remotely teaching us from another location all the information that we need, stage by stage, to help us to successfully complete the course. Each lesson that we successfully complete prepares us for the next one, where we build on the last, and so forth. When we've successfully completed the lessons in the course, we are equipped and qualified to go out and do the work of our dream job. Pretty easy to follow right? Well that is exactly how our walk with God is.

God allows us to go through certain situations in life to teach and equip us with what we need for some future life situation. Unfortunately many of us we don't seek out God's guidance in His Word, but instead make decisions based on our own limited wisdom and desires. These often lead us into unnecessary detours, unnecessary relationships, and painful relationships. Even less dramatic, they often just lead us into unfulfilling jobs and life routines that leave us feeling empty. However, God's Word says that His Word is useful for teaching us what we need to know, correcting us where we've gone wrong and training us in the right decisions to make (2 Timothy 3:16). If we consulted the Word sooner we'd have been better set up and perhaps in a fraction of the time. However, we should not feel condemned as God in all His grace and mercy uses the situations we have been through to teach us empathy, the power of grace and quite frankly the paucity of our own knowledge about figuring out life. God will use those experiences we went through to equip us to help and empower others. No experience is wasted. As we go through the series of lessons, keep the faith and complete the course we are equipped to go out into the world and fulfil the purpose for which God has created us.

That purpose in the context of destiny is the unique assignment for which God created us. This is the ultimate goal—to fulfil the purpose for which we have been created. However if we don't take the time to consciously tune into Skye to gain the knowledge and wisdom from our Teacher in dealing with our life lessons and situations, we will end up doing things our own way and going round and round in circles as we end up making mistakes and wasting valuable time. Surely now that our eyes are open we don't want to do this! We don't want to continue doing things our way because God's way is way too challenging to our faith? That's exactly what the Children of Israel did when God delivered them from Egypt. God's plan was to prepare them in advance so that they could inhabit the Promised Land of Canaan, living according to His will. In order to teach them the lessons God took them on a journey. The journey should have only taken 11 days, but because they didn't want to listen, obey and trust God, they ended up doing their own thing, making up idols and false gods. In this journey they were so set and stubborn about doing things their own way that they ended up wasting time by completing an 11-day journey in a total 40 years! Why? Because every time they didn't listen and obey God they continued to walk in the wilderness around the same mountain time and time again.

God has prepared an awesome purpose and destiny waiting for us, and the more attentive we are to submitting our lives to Him and trusting Him along our live path, the less time we will waste in going round and round in circles to learn the same life lessons.

Part of the lesson we will have to learn is how to embrace being confident in being different. Living for God means that we will be different from the world. We'll behave differently and live our lives differently. God's Word says that we are to come out from the world and be different (2 Corinthians 6:17). This means that on a day to day basis we will need to be familiar enough with God's Word that we can have confidence in it and in Him that when He says to have faith and trust Him in our life situations that we will do just that, even if it means doing things differently to what is customary to the people around us.

Everything the world does is according to man's logic and reasoning. It requires little to no faith and is the safe and comfortable route because we can count on ourselves that things will go according to our plan if we follow the logical plan we've prepared. However God's plan was not for our souls to leave eternity and come into this life to forsake the great plan and destiny that He created for us. He doesn't want us to depend on our own wisdom and knowledge and come up with our own plans of doing things. Our God is a big and phenomenal

God. His plans are magnificent, look at how He made the universe, the planets and all the wonders of the world. Why would we choose to sell ourselves short by forsaking God's plan to make up our own plan which could not compare and would be far more inferior. Yet this is what happens every single day in life. The world generally has such little understanding of God and His purposes and is clouded by mankind's reasoning and logic that every day people choose their own plan instead of building a relationship with our Creator God and seeking out His plan, purpose and destiny for our lives.

Because God's power and plans are beyond the capacity of our human reasoning and understanding, when He tells us to do things it generally has certain characteristics that we tend not to understand. His plans usually make no sense, sound impossible and often make us feel way out of our depth. The reason why? God's plans require us to have faith and trust in Him and His Word.

It takes faith when we're in the midst of bewildering circumstances to believe that God has planned, prepared and already worked out every step of our life path for our good. Committing to a lifestyle of faith makes us different from the average person, who follows logical reasoning. God requires us to follow His Word and the leading of His Holy Spirit. Following God like this requires us to develop a bold courageousness to be comfortable in being different to the crowd, and having confidence in walking in unchartered waters. We can only do this if we truly believe and trust God and the visions that He has entrusted us with. We cannot proceed successfully if we're preoccupied analysing the situations around us like everyone else, we have to be comfortable being different. The bible says it this way:

> *Do not conform to the pattern of this world, but be transformed by the renewing of your mind. Then you will be able to test and approve what God's will is—his good, pleasing and perfect will.* —Romans 12:2

The more regularly we follow God's word and trust Him with our life situations, the more we will see His presence manifest in working out our life situations in often unconceivable ways. Seeing God's hand in our everyday lives is what increases our faith. Seeing Him move in the lives of the people connected to us emboldens us to keep trusting Him in our own lives. Consistently living by faith through all life's lessons, the situations and trials helps to build our faith and reliance on God. Over time, just as in our skype lesson analogy, we become equipped with godly wisdom through all life's lessons to live a fulfilled life whilst we live out the very purpose for which we were created.

REMEMBERING THAT WE DON'T KNOW

Often times in every day life we get stuck and frustrated trying to figure everything out. What we have to remember is that some situations are deliberately brought into our life for the very reasons that we cannot figure them out. Our job is not to figure it out, but to exercise our faith in God by following His Word to allow life to unfold the exact way that God has ordained it to align with a plan that works out in ways that only He knows. This is not always easy, and especially when we are living in a different realm to the analogous Teacher, and particularly in the midst of tests. To be completely honest it's quite easy to slip back into our comfort zone mode of trying to figure things out for ourselves. It takes a significant amount of discipline to develop the habit of tuning out of this busy world and its mindset, and settling into the calm stillness of our skype connection with God to receive guidance, comfort and wisdom on taking the next steps of our life path.

The more habitually we devote time to read, study and apply the principles of God's Word to our lives, the more we will begin to develop our relationship with Him and recognise how He works in the minute details of our lives. Often times we overlook the synchronicity that God has ordered in our life events, which we tend to pass over as 'a coincidence'. These are not random events in our lives, they are the manifestation of God's providence where He prepared a set of instances to happen at the exact same and all to benefit us. That's how big and reliable our God is! When we become more mindful and conscious of recognising God in these everyday life situations it encourages us to develop along this journey of faith into destiny.

TRICKY SITUATIONS

The tricky bit in everyday life is mastering the technique of self-control over our thoughts and behaviours. Sometimes we find ourselves in life situations where we literally feel we're about to drown, and the worst part is that in seeking out God, He appears to be silent, or worse still absent. If we're not careful to get a hold on our emotions, we can run away with feelings of fearfulness and abandonment. But that's not from God because He said that He will never leave us nor forsake us. He is with us every step of the way. Sometimes the storms come just to test where our faith is; This was the case when Jesus was in the boat with His followers. The storm came and they cried out in terror that they were going to drown. They didn't have the faith to believe that with Jesus in the boat there was no need to fear perilous times of storms. If they truly believed in Jesus' power they'd have confidently woken Him to command the storm to cease. Of course Jesus could have calmed the sea, for He is the living breathing Word of God and thus any single thing or situation that the Word of God commands, has to obey. I believe that God allowed this situation with Jesus and his followers to take place as an example for as much to them as it is to us to encourage us in our own walk of faith. There will be times that we will find ourselves amongst the storms of life. We now know it is our responsibility not to get caught up in the drama of the situation, but to focus our attention on God's Word. That shift in focus calms our mind, encourages our faith and enables us to trust with confidence that as we pray and commit our situations into God's hands that He is faithful to direct us and lead us into right paths for our lives. We need to become accustomed to seeing tests not as inconveniences, but as opportunities to grow, change and evolve into our destiny.

• • •

CHAPTER FOUR

SURRENDER

"God's way. God's timing. God's plan".

WHAT IT MEANS TO SURRENDER

Changing the way that we live and make decisions to totally rely on God's Word. It takes a phenomenal amount of courage and strength. This is because it means that we have to leave our comfort zones and surrender control, the very thing that usually gives us some assurance of peace of mind *"if I can just get everything under my control, it will all be okay".* But says who? We often fool ourselves into believing that we have more power than we actually do, and often times it takes sudden tragedies to remind us of how little control we have over anything in the big scheme of life. Literally, anything good, bad or indifferent can happen in an instant. Therefore truth be told surrendering is counterintuitive to our normal modus operandi and is one of the single biggest challenges when we journey on this walk of faith along the life path that God has created for us.

So what does it actually mean to surrender control to God? This baffled me for such a long time as a Christian, probably because I used to be such a control freak! Surrendering to God simply means that we make a conscious decision to give up the ideas of how *we think life should be*, or how *we think* situations should turn out, and instead follow God's principles for life and thereafter allow life to take its natural course and just flow with it. It means not wrestling or manipulating situations (or people) to turn out the way that we want them to, but instead trusting that our obedience in applying God's principles to our lives means that He will ensure that everything we *need* is already taken care of. It's trusting that no matter the outcome of a situation, once we have done what we know we are supposed to do, God has already worked out the situation so that whatever happens and wherever we end up, we will be exactly where God intended us to be, perfectly aligned in His will. That's trusting God's providence, and is at the crux of surrender as we walk our life path.

In real terms, surrender means that whilst we won't be able to have that comfortable predictable outcome that we'd like, we can rest perfectly assured that once we've done our bit in obedience we have really leave it in God's hands. I said God! Not just anybody who can disappoint us, I said God! God who is faithful to His Word. God who created the entire universe, and knows the very situation we are in. God who has engraved us on the palms of His hands (Isaiah 49:16) who watches over every word He has spoken over our life to ensure that it is performed (Jeremiah 1:12). God the Way-Maker who went before the children of Israel and in parted the waters so they had a route to escape from their enemies. God who has put a hedge of protection around those obedient to His word to limit the enemy's access to you (Job 1:9-10). When we remind ourselves that we are trusting the Almighty, All Powerful, All Knowing God we can trust a lot more easier. This is also what it means by counting your blessings. When we remember all the things God has done for us and all the situations that He has protected us from and delivered us out of, we can be assured that He will do it again for our God is faithful and He loves us dearly.

Here's an example from my own life on the lesson of surrender; I was temping at a job I had been at for almost a year. My Manager approached me with her second attempt to get me to become a permanent member of staff, but this time within a different team. It was clear that if I wanted the job it would be mine. She set up a meeting with the Manager of my prospective team and the pitch was perfect. The job sounded like everything I wanted. They were offering me all the flexibility that I had said I needed, and all I had to do was say the word and the job would be mine. Except one thing, something didn't feel right. I couldn't explain it but I just didn't feel the peace of God. It made no logical sense as on paper it was everything I wanted, but for some reason God's peace was not there. So, ignoring everything in the natural, and let me expand on what that meant—ignoring the seemingly perfect job, my needs for a stable and regular income, I decided to trust God who leads with His peace, which was not there in that seemingly perfect job offer. That Philippians 4:7 peace that transcends all understanding that was missing. And in trusting God I took that courageous leap of faith and notified my Manager a week or so later in the loveliest rejection letter that sadly I would not be able to proceed with the job being offered. I'm just going to keep it all the way real. In the intervening week from the meeting to my letter, I really pressed into God to explain something to me, because nothing made sense. The Manager was offering me everything I asked for. Then God put it on my spirit that if the manager left employment, or the offices relocated, then what would have seemed like the perfect job would become a colossal nightmare. I thought to myself what a random set of circumstances it would take for either to happen. Then, after tendering my letter my manager stopped speaking to me. I didn't know what to do. I had tried to be obedient and I ended up finding myself in this unpleasant situation. I asked my manager for a meeting as I wanted to clear up the air and make sure that I wasn't going to be fired. She was guarded but assured me that she'd give me plenty of notice if they had to let me go to fill my post permanently. Then as God would have it, a week later my manager came to me and told me that it was a good thing that I didn't apply for the job because the person who would have been my manager had tendered his resignation, and the offices were relocating! Imagine that! At that point absolutely everything made sense. I understood in retrospect that having faith in God means that I need to make peace with the fact that I will often not be able to make sense of what's happening in the moment, but that really doesn't matter because God is omnipresent—He's in the past, present and the future and has arranged every situation in our lives to work together perfectly so that we don't end up in situations that look good to us but leave us in difficulties further down the path. This path of faith is full of parts we just cannot see further down. All we can do is use the principles of God's Word to light and direct our feet along our path and trust that where we end up further down the path is for our good. God did say that the plans He has for us are for our good and not evil, so we just need to trust Him on that (Jeremiah 29:11). These are the situations that come our way to test our faith in God, and when we pass that lesson, there's often a blessing and it's onto the next until we complete the course. I can see now being way down that path that God had it all perfectly worked out for me. Not long after my manager told me the offices were relocating, I was contacted by my agency to take a job so close home I could literally walk it to work within fifteen minutes, whereas the other job was an hours commute each way. Needless to say I got the job near home, and as they say the rest is history! We serve a mighty and faithful God and if we want to see Him move in our lives we have to trust Him.

GOD'S PLANS ARE FOR OUR GOOD

The principle is quite simple; Live according to God's Word and trust that the outcome is God's destined will, and in time we will see the bigger picture. However when we add life's circumstances and human emotion into the mix it makes things seem far more complicated. However every time that we surrender and vulnerably trust the power of God's Word, He is absolutely faithful to work things out for our good. It's at those times when we feel that we're at our weakest because we have no control that God manifests in the midst of our life situations and makes us strong and steady by faithfully showing up and working things out on our behalf for our good. And this doesn't just work for situations, it also works for our soul. When we surrender to God in our most shameful state, God is faithful and patient to guide us to work through our situations and through His healing grace He helps us to transform into the image He created us to be, clothing us with His dignity and strength. Through the steady process of time we will emerge from our situations of brokenness into a state of wholeness and strength. God literally uses our life situations to mould us into the person He's created us to become and prepare us for the purpose for which we've been created. Going through this process is a witness to the people around us of God's power, and the power of His Word when we put our trust in it and live by it. Each test becomes a testimony as we keep walking and trusting God along our journey of faith up our life path.

THE PROCESS OF GROWTH INTO DESTINY

A life submitted to God can be likened to the process of stripping away of all the cocoon-type layers around our soul. These analogous cocoon layers have been gradually formed by living our lives from the time we were born according to the world's ways of doing things. The life decisions and habits we've formed during that time were probably not aligned with God's Word. With every bad decision and habit we formed a cocoon-like barrier over our soul and acting as a barrier to our communication with God. The consequence of this barrier forming is that we grow and go through life without a living relationship with God. We grow without a consciousness of His presence and our soul ends up travelling up the paths of life in this dark world without the guidance from the light of God's Word to direct our path (Psalm 119:105). Instead we rely on our own wisdom and the customs of the world. Our soul is trapped in this shell as we walk in darkness along our life's paths. We don't know what's right for our life according to God's plan because we have no real personal relationship with Him so we just follow what the customs of the world to dictate our life trajectory. Eventually we become restless and yearn for a sense of freedom and fulfilment. This is often the catalyst to our soul-searching journey for the meaning of life.

As we seek out God and apply the principles of His Word to our lives, we begin to slowly break free from that cocoon-type barrier which separates us from enjoying a personal relationship with God and achieving our destiny. The more we surrender the more we begin shedding each layer. Slowly over the process of time and surrender cracks appear in the cocoon and the light of God's Word begins to shine into our soul to guide us along our predestined life path. The sheer power of this process builds our faith which empowers us to continue surrendering and breaking free through the layers. The cocoon-layers we shed are symbolic of the false narratives that we've been taught as the way to live life—they're the world's customs but not God's way. The more we begin to live according to God's Word the more we gain the strength to transform out of the cocoon and into the image of the person God created us to be. We shed our old mindsets and habits from states of brokenness into wholeness, in oneness with God thinking and living according to His Word.

Through this metamorphic process we break free from the cocoon layers and emerge as a completely different and whole person like a beautiful butterfly ready to take flight in the world, spreading our wings to live and fulfil the divine purpose for which God created us so we can experience true fulfilment in life.

* * *

CHAPTER FIVE

GROWING PAINS

"In order to grow we have to change. But change isn't comfortable or easy. It can be painful".

BE REALISTIC AND PATIENT

Reading about the transformation process is one thing, but actually living it well that's a whole other story. As creatures of habit we feel both comfortable and secure in familiar territory. Change generally tends to make most of us feel uncomfortable, even anxious. Familiarity feels like stability. However life with God requires us to transform completely out of that mind-set because growth in Him involves a constant state of evolution through stages of growth and change. As we know, walking our life path with God requires faith because it requires us walking along unknown and unfamiliar paths. Whist the situations are probably the same every day situations, the way we approach them in being committed to God's principles is what makes it unfamiliar. We've seen that God rarely reveals the details; He usually gives a Word to follow or gives us a revelation by some prophetic means. Whatever the prophetic revelation is, will require faith as it's going to look impossible, dare I even say crazy to the logical mind. Just like Jesus told Peter to come out of the boat and walk on water to Him, that's the same type of faith it's going to take for us to step out of our own comfort zones and walk having faith in His Word.

Another real emotion we'll feel at some point in our walk of faith is fear. And that's okay. It's okay to feel the fear, it's a normal human emotion when entering unfamiliar territory. What we do have to master though is not *giving in to the fear*. It's a lesson of courage that we have to go through time and time again in different forms to build up our faith muscles—feeling fear, admitting it and facing it and obeying God anyway. Honestly in some situations it's normal to feel the desire to want to abandon the faith and take back control over our lives, particularly when we're in our infancy stages of our walk with God. It's not a check-box exercise, it's a growth process which takes time over many different situations. We build our faith muscle to give us the strength to courageously go *through* these situations when we feel fear by taking the time to read and study His Word. The more familiar with God's Word, the more familiar we are with His character in all types of situations, and believe there are many in the bible to see the character of God! Whether it's David setting up situations for a man to be killed in order to take his wife (2 Samuel 11) or the desperation of a woman dealing with seeming infertility (Genesis 16). Even how to deal with endless trials (Job 1). When we become familiar with how God relates to each person in the bible and how He is so involved in the intricacies of their life situations, it helps us to understand the principles of God to enable us to apply them to our own life situations. And not just know God principles, but be filled with faith that just as God was faithfully involved in their situations that He has total divine control over our own. This is why it's so important to take the time to regularly spend time reading and reflecting on the bible. We learn how sometimes God will respond with grace, and sometimes He will require us to deal with the consequences of our actions. As we spend regular time immersing our mind in God's Word, it begins to shift our own mind-sets and stimulates our faith to grow. This gives us the necessary confidence and courage to exercise our faith in times of our own trials. In the midst of any storm we need to be familiar enough with God to be able to put our trust and hope in Him. And as we've seen that courage comes from having a strong knowledge of God in our hearts, from reading His Word and all the countless situations He rescued His people who put their trust in Him against all the odds. That kind of faith and growth is not something that we can do in our own natural strength. As we've seen through the cocoon example, it's the light and strength of God's Word that helps us break through all our layers to grow into the image and destiny God created us for.

And the obvious question is what about when we fall? When we can't bring ourselves to follow God's Word in whatever situation we're going through? We need to remember this, none of us are perfect. Sometimes we're going to miss it because that's exactly what sin is—missing the mark of what we're suppose to do. If we are genuinely trying to obey God and we miss the mark, God says His grace is sufficient for us (2 Corinthians 12:9). That's a different situation to when we know very well what to do and intend in our heart to do something completely different to God's word. That's not missing it, that's wilfully disobeying God. Now I'm not going to feign any type of holiness because we are all human and have done things we're not proud of. But what we know from God's Word is that He is just. He gives grace when the situation requires it, and He allows the repercussions of our decisions at times also. However what we can be certain of is that God is balanced, He never goes over the top and makes us go through more than necessary, and He never ever leaves or abandons us because He loves us too much.

So when we do fall, we have to get back up again because the righteous man falls seven times and gets back up again (Proverbs 24:16). When we get back up we need to go before God with a truly sorry heart and repent to Him. There's no need to wallow in condemnation. If we're truly sorry and repentant God is faithful to forgive us, and so we must forgive ourselves (1 John 1:9). And thus the life and the growth process goes on no matter how many times we fall. Contrary to what some people would try and have you believe, God does not relish in punishing us. We are His masterpiece! He took time and great care to create us. He knew our souls from before we came into this world and loves us deeply. He is rooting for us to succeed through our trials and situations so that we can become the image of who He created us to be and live the destined plans He has prepared for us. He won't give up on us, so we can't give up on Him. (Ephesians 1:11)

WHEN WE MAKE MISTAKES

One of the enemy's greatest weapons to stop us exercising our faith in God is to give us feelings of guilt. When we make mistakes and fall, if we are not quick to repent and correct our mind-set in alignment with God's Word, the enemy will surely tempt us with thoughts of guilt that fill our minds with condemnation. This is all an effort to try to convince us that we are beyond the help and grace of God. However this is most certainly not true. God knows that we have a whole lifestyle of habits and behaviours to change, and He is very patient with us through the process. Let's not forget that it took the children of Israel 40 years travelling in the wilderness to adjust their mind-sets, and yet God was with them all the way. He didn't abandon them on the journey. He remained faithfully with them and brought the faithful ones into the promised land of Canaan. The same is true for our lives along this transformational journey. God is patient with us and never leaves us. There will be some areas that we will triumph over far easier than others.

STRONGHOLDS

Many of us have some longstanding deep-rooted issues to deal with as a result of things we've gone through in life. Often times without godly wisdom and/or professional guidance or therapy, we deal with these through dysfunctional coping mechanisms that result in self-destructive behaviours. One such example could be the effects of having an absent father figure in our lives without a sufficient buffer of love to counteract that loss. This can cause some women to seek out love in the form of relationships. Sadly there are men who see a woman's vulnerability and exploit it by treating them disrespectfully. When we have unmet and unaddressed needs in our lives, we settle for things that are less than God's best for us in a desperate attempt to have our needs met. This is why we have to be careful to be mentally and emotionally at our optimal state before trying to offer anything to anyone in a relationship. By entering relationships when we're not emotionally whole leaves us susceptible to forming toxic and dysfunctional emotional bonds that can cause trauma bonds, co-dependency and pain. Unfortunately, instead of such relationships building us up into our best selves, they exploit our vulnerabilities and bring out the worst in us and sometimes create situations that are difficult to undo.

DEEP NEEDS

Everyone is different and reaches for different things to satisfy or mask their unmet needs, but effectively they are all emotional or physical crutches that we've used to try and help us get through life. We now know that this is not God's will. God's Word is our benchmark in what standard we should be trying to attain in being emotionally healthy. Sometimes however the issues we've been through are so deeply painful that it may require professional help such as a Counsellor or Therapist, and that is okay too. God has equipped each person in life with a gift to be able to use in service for His work to help others (Exodus 35:35). Therefore there is nothing wrong and actually a very good decision to seek professional help when dealing with deep-rooted difficulties. God has equipped professional people with the skills to be able to help us through whatever we're facing. The first step toward that life transformational change is facing the truth about what is not working in our lives. This itself can be challenging, but like the seedling pushing itself up through the dirt into growth, we must do the same.

As stated above, the first stage of moving in the right direction requires us to recognise and admit where we are not aligned with God's will/Word. In the example above, it requires an acceptance that it is not God's will for any of us to be partnered with someone who is not building us up in God's holiness and wholeness. It takes phenomenal strength and courage to walk away from things that we have become deeply emotionally bonded to. Surrendering means placing those things, our emotional crutches on the altar of surrender, and walking away trusting that God will support us without those crutches. This is not always easy and sometimes we will hit a weak spot. Weak spots are the points where we're tempted to return to the altar and take back our emotional crutches, even though we know it's not God's will. Even at times like this, as long as we maintain our relationship with God we will feel convicted by God's Holy Spirit when we are doing things that are not according to God's Word/will. God is so gracious that He gives us other opportunities to surrender and walk away from these things. It is a process, and God's Word says that His grace is sufficient for us because His power is made perfect when we are in our weakness (2 Corinthians 12:9). This is why we must not succumb to guilty thoughts that make us feel that we cannot get back into relationship with God. God doesn't give up on a heart that longs for Him, so if we fall we have to just get back up again. We must be realistic and accept that we will make mistakes, and when we do God's Word says:

> *Let us then approach God's throne of grace with confidence, so that we may receive mercy and find grace to help us in our time of need.* —Hebrews 4:16

When we fall we are to approach God in all sincerity being sorry for our mistakes. It means we have to re-focus and place our trust and hope in His Word to keep us from going backwards and down a path of destruction. That said, it is also important that we absolutely must not treat the grace of God with contempt and disrespect. If we begin to wilfully and repeatedly do things that we know to be wrong without a repentant heart we are treading on very dangerous territory. We do not want God to take away His Holy Spirit from us. That results in permanent separation from Him, and is the sure path to eternal destruction.

ENOUGH IS ENOUGH

The great thing about God is that He knows exactly what each of us needs to drive us to the place of humility. That place where we stop wrestling with God in order to live life 'our way' but instead decide *enough is enough!* It's that place where we reach our wits ends because we're sick and tired of being sick and tired of anything that's holding us back from making progress in our lives. It's at that point that we're usually ready and willing to surrender to God the most difficult parts of our lives. No it's not easy. As we have seen we will probably make mistakes (sometimes multiple times) but ultimately if our hearts and minds are toward God and we are truly seeking change, God will empower us to overcome. It is all a part of the growing and transformation process. We now know that the critical step is first developing that strong intimate relationship with God through getting to know Him through spending time learning His ways in different situations in the bible. This empowers us to change. We have to be patient with both ourselves and the transformational growth process.

TRUSTING GOD

Developing a strong confidence in God comes by going through a myriad of experiences where we have decided to trust Him. The more we trust Him the more He will show us through our life situations that He is faithfully remaining with us to guide us to the best decisions for our lives. We know His will when we understand the principles of His ways as detailed in the bible, and know how to apply it in our everyday life situations.

When we're walking through trials of faith, trusting God means applying His Word to our lives and then surrendering. It means trusting His timing and also trusting that His outcome will manifest out of the situation we're trusting Him with. No, it is not always easy. Sometimes in life God will take us through seasons of silence after we've surrendered a situation to Him. In those moments it can feel like quite a bewildering experience. We don't know what's happening and the trial often seems to last forever. I know, I've been there! Now consider this: Sometimes God's outcome is not the outcome we would have expected, and if we're truly honest it's not the outcome we want to accept either. Trusting God doesn't just mean trusting the process, it also means trusting the outcome. It means that having submitted to His Word, whatever the outcome is, that is what God intended it to be, even if we don't like it. What I have learned is that as time goes on, sometimes we will begin to understand why certain situations were necessary in our lives, and essential to our growth. We may not always like these experiences, but oftentimes they are the very situations that precipitate the greatest chapters of growth in our lives. They are hallmark experiences and defining moments in our lives that have a way of refining our character to change us into the person that God destined us to be. This means that we can effectively fulfil our purpose in life.

UNEXPECTED OUTCOMES

The most challenging part in all of this is when we experience unexpected outcomes. This can be difficult to endure as they often leave us feeling out of control in life, and we can't necessarily see the direction that things will take. At times like this we must remember the greatness and powerfulness of our God. He exists in a realm far higher than ours in eternity, from which He has already planned and worked out how all of our life circumstances will work out together for our good. God exists outside of time. When He created the earth, He created time to govern it. Time governs seasons on earth, it does not govern God, for He governs it. This helps us to understand that when God created our life path, He did so knowing the beginning, the end and everything in between. He has indeed already gone before us in time to prepare our way. We are the ones that are late to the party. The paucity of our human understanding cannot even begin to conceive of God's plans and how He will work things out.

We will begin to experience a far more enjoyable life when we learn to stop trying to be the co-pilot of our lives. God doesn't need a co-pilot, He is the Pilot and can more than handle the task of guiding along our life path. As we surrender our lives to God, we have to trust that wherever that journey takes us is absolutely God's will and exactly where we are meant to be. God is the Pilot who navigates our life journey, and His plans for us are for our good and not for evil regardless of whatever we see with our natural eyes, or even the emotions that we feel. We cannot and must not prioritise and put them higher than our faith in God and His word. If we are truly submitted to Him, then we are under the submission of His Word, not our emotions, not how we think we should figure out the situation according to our own wisdom. No! God is the surest navigational system that we can trust and when He directs us through the application of His Word and through prayer, we cannot fail. Yes sometimes it may look scary, or the odds may look against us. When you place your hope in God's Word it is impossible to fail.

THE LIFE OF JOB

Think about Job; He put all his trust and hope in God. When the storms of life hit, it looked like his entire life was falling apart. Even his wife and friends thought that he was finished. But he wasn't, and in fact Job didn't even do anything wrong. The storm and calamity was just a trial that God allowed to come into Job's life to give him a unique opportunity to exercise and develop his faith and relationship with God. And because God knew that Job would be faithful through it all, He used Job as an example to satan to show the faithfulness of God's servant. After Job successfully completed this trial, God not only restored what he lost, but God gave him *double for his trouble!* (Job 42:10).

...

CHAPTER SIX

FAILURE

"Failure isn't final. It is simply the rungs of lessons we climb on the ladder in our journey to success."

As we grow in God it becomes necessary for us to renew our mind-sets about certain things. One such area is our perspective on 'failure'. In its traditional sense failure is when we don't accomplish a particular aim or purpose in the way that we've had in our mind.

When we decide to surrender our lives to God, this means also surrendering what and how we have planned and conceived our purposes and plans. It certainly does not mean that we abandon our dreams and goals. Surrendering simply means that we submit them to God to see whether they are acceptable to Him. This helps us to be sure that our plans are in alignment with His will for our lives. Now let's be clear, that's not to say that God doesn't allow us to pursue our passions or desires. Of course He does. In fact God delights and wills for us to use the passions and gifts that He gave us so that we can serve His purposes and show His love to others in service. It's less about using them and more about *the purpose* for which we use them. We can and should be faithful and good stewards of the life and gifts that God has given us. Surrendering in this context means that as we go ahead and plan our lives, we should be seeking out the mind and will of God on our proposed plans. When our plans align with His will they are automatically blessed with peace and success. There is nothing that God would want us to do that would contradict His Word or cause us to forfeit our God-given destiny, so it is in our best interest to seek Him first and go the way that is blessed, even if it looks strange or like failure. God's Word says that man plans his ways but God directs His path. So we can go ahead and plan but we must take it to God so He can direct us whether this is the way we should be going or not.

Sometimes we need examples to drive the point home; Imagine a woman thriving and doing exceptionally well in her career. Her boss may lead her to believe that in order to go even higher up the career ladder, she would have to compromise her Christian values and do something underhanded that would not align with the principles of God's Word. Such an opportunity is not of God because any opportunity sent by God will not require us to compromise His Word or sell our soul to attain it. Similarly sometimes in life we greatly desire something, but for whatever reason it seems elusive and it's just not working out for us. Or even maybe things are working out but deep down in our hearts we know that this is not the path we should be taking. Either way we can know whether we're on the right path based on whether it takes aligns with God's will, and if we experience His peace. Sometimes God will give us a clear indication when our plans are not in His will and we just have to accept it. The bible says that unless the Lord builds our house (life) we will labour in vain. This means that if the woman in the example above decides to engage in compromising behaviour, she is compromising God's Word in her life and therefore she should not succumb to the tempting offer.

God gives us His Holy Spirit to guide us into making right decisions. When we ignore these warnings and gentle nudges of the Holy Spirit, we can very ignorantly and stubbornly cause ourselves to fall into sin and end up in destructive situations over and over again. This will keep happening until we learn the lesson that God is trying to teach us through our life situations. Instead of making progress, we can end up going round in vicious circles, walking around that proverbial mountain as the children of Israel did for forty years because they refused to submit to God's word and way of living. Instead of us being so rigidly affixed to our own plans, our first plan should be to take our desires to God to seek His direction on them to see if they are in His will, and to seek guidance on the path that we are supposed to take. This is what it means that we are to trust in the Lord with all our hearts and lean not to our understanding. In *all of our ways* and our plans we are to submit to Him (for His approval, guidance and direction) and when we do that, God is faithful to direct us along our rightful life path. That is the path full of godly opportunities, divine connections and open doors waiting for us to courageously walk towards and through in fulfilling the good plans God has for us along our life path.

And what if we don't listen and obey God's guidance? Well much like the children of Israel we could end up going round in circles in our life. That's one of the lesser of two not so great outcomes. The other outcome happened to Saul in 1 Chronicles 10. His ego became so enlarged that his focus became less and less on God and more on the things around him. Those things began to influence his mind, his mood and his ego. Eventually he was unfaithful to God. He didn't follow God's guidance as King and so in verse 13-14 we see that he completely lost his path by trying to do things his way and ended up dead. There is great importance in obeying and submitting to God because His Word and guidance bring life and set us up on the right life paths. However as the bible says, the wages of sin is death (Romans 6:23), and so we really need to prioritise and develop the practice of just obeying God and trusting His plan and guidance the very first time we receive that guidance.

A GOOD STEWARD

God has given each of us certain talents and He does not want us to be reckless with the life and talents that He has given us. We are supposed to nourish and develop passions and become a spiritually, physically and economically fruitful people so that we can reach out and be a blessing to others throughout our lives sharing the love of God. Therefore after seeking to develop a deep and personal relationship with God, our life goal should be to find out the plan God has for us to use our lives and talents, and commit ourselves to that purpose; That is what we were born for!

ROADBLOCKS AND UNEXPECTED OCCURRENCES ON OUR PATH

At times we'll make decisions based on what we think is the right course of action, and then we may become discouraged when it looks like things are not working out. We should not be discouraged especially when we hit roadblocks. Sometimes God allows them to show up in our lives to specifically stop us from continuing down a particular path. In the moment, that roadblock can be real challenging because it looks like it's blocking a great plan or opportunity. What we often fail to realise is that God has seen the end of that path and knows that it isn't in fact good and doesn't lead us into the destiny that He has created for us; A destiny which is far greater and better than any plans that we have formed in our own minds. In those situations roadblocks are God's way of ushering us into the direction that we are supposed to go, even if it doesn't look like it at the time. At times like these we need to practice the art of surrendering to God.

We have to keep reminding ourselves that on this faith journey, we are to walk by faith and not by sight. Not everything will make sense to our natural eyes and perception. The plans and wisdom of God come from the unseen realm that exists outside of earth. Therefore we cannot expect to understand God's wisdom with our eyes or human reasoning. Some things are only understood in hindsight, and quite often that is how we come to understand that roadblocks are actually blessings in disguise. This is how we adjust our perception of failure. Think about how many times we've heard people say "*If it hadn't been for this or that happening, such and such would never have happened!*". We are often left astonished when we look back in retrospect and see how the Hand of God has moved in our lives.

As people living a faith lifestyle submitted to God, we have to adjust how we perceive roadblocks and what may seem like failure. If we don't succeed in some event or plan that God never intended for us to be a part of, that really isn't failure! In fact if we have resisted the urge to manipulate situations and people to try and succeed in our plan, and have decided to surrender to the flow of life, what we'll find out at some point is that where Life takes us is in fact exactly where God wanted us to be and ultimately what is best for us. We rarely see and recognise that in real time, and this is why it's a journey of faith. We recognise it more clearly when we look back and can connect the dots. Until then we literally have to exercise our trust and faith in God that everything that happens in our lives is happening *for us*, and for our good. In one moment a certain situation may look like failure, but with the benefit of godly insight and foresight we can see how the seeming failure was actually a blessing in disguise. Sometimes our most blessed situations can be borne out of painful or challenging circumstances. I often remind myself that pressure produces diamonds. Therefore in such moments of bewilderment it is necessary to exercise self-control and calm our minds from racing with all kinds of thoughts.

Another thing we need to be conscious of is that God will not allow any situation to come to us without a reason. No matter how bad things may seem God has allowed them to come to us and arranged in such a way that they are all happening *for our good*. As we've already seen, once we have applied God's Word to our lives we have to be still and simply allow ourselves to flow through whatever life path God's leads us into, trusting that all things will work together for our good. (Romans 8:28)

In short, our job is to seek God's will to navigate us into taking the best next best step in our life path. Once we receive that guidance we are required to follow it through regardless of whether it makes sense to us. Living like this requires us to repeatedly practice taking faith-filled steps whilst surrendering to the flow of life's events. Although challenging, we have to keep walking by faith with the assurance even though we don't know how things will turn out, God has arranged the outcome to work out for our good. That's our assurance and the only one we need.

...

CHAPTER SEVEN

SUCCESS IS...

When we think about destiny, it often evokes ideals in our minds of things that we aspire to achieve—*that ideal job, home, husband or wife* and the list goes on. I mean let's be real, nobody wants to live a life that doesn't excel in any way. With that in mind, we tend to see success as our ideal destination in life, a place where we've '*made it*' and achieved our life ambitions. But is that really what success is? Did God, in all His infinite wisdom simply create us to fulfil a checklist of goals?

There's definitely no doubt that achievement feels good. But is this feeling (as good as it is) enduring and satisfying? Does it truly fulfil us? If we're totally honest, the answer is no. It's only temporary; We're happy, celebratory and are so excited to share our great feeling. However, in a short amount of time the regular humdrum of life sets in. We're thankful for our achievement but it somehow just fits into our ordinary world, and we carry on. It may mean we carry on with a better salary, improved career, or even more comfortable lifestyle. Those things are exterior to our soul. They make life (and our ego) feel good, but internally in the depths of our soul it eventually becomes business as usual as we strive towards our next goal because typically the more we get the more we want. In this context, success is a state of acquisition (of goals and achievements) that hallmark our progress in life. It does good for our cultural acceptance and our egos, but is limited in its power to empower us with fulfilment. Yet, what we're all fundamentally seeking after at our core is fulfilment. It's that place where our thoughts, our emotions and the living being of our soul are all perfectly aligned in a unified sense of completeness. That completeness is intrinsically linked to our fulfilment of purpose.

Most of us have been so deeply influenced by society's culture of equating success with purpose that we spend the vast majority of our lives trying to achieve a list of ideals in order to validate our existence. However, we now know that God was intentional about creating our lives, and as such our purpose far exceeds any goals that we set for ourselves. Our purpose is bigger than the frame of our individual life, for it is interlinked and interwoven in the bigger picture of destiny to the world around us. We have been divinely placed on earth at this time, in this space to play a specific role in the big scheme of life, in ways that only we can because that is how God so equipped us. Our skills, personality, all those idiosyncrasies that make us unique are the very tools God has given us to impact the world. But it's tough because the world culture celebrates conformity and to be different, unique and individual risks isolation, rejection and exclusion. Differences are rarely celebrated in humble beginnings, yet that is the seedling form of destiny. And so, instead of us feeling empowered to nurture and celebrate our differences, we hide them and downplay them in a bid to fit in and feel an acceptable part of society. We would do good to remember that the trailblazers in life are not the ones who quietly slipped into the order of normality. They're the ones who stepped out of line, dared to take a risk for what they believed in and pursued a dream and purpose that so fundamentally resonated with their being that meant more to them than fitting in, or quitting. It drove them to persevering difficulties and setbacks and eventually when they fulfilled their dream the world caught up to realise the vision that was all along embedded in their soul. That's purpose and that's what pursuit of purpose will cost.

As seen above, the journey to fulfilment is not one easily tread. It forces us to search and connect with the innermost parts of ourselves, which is something that most people find extremely difficult. Connecting with ourselves essentially means that we stand face to face with the essence of who we are and what we believe to the core of our soul. It's where we come face to face with our fears, weaknesses and vulnerabilities. It's an uncomfortable process because in pursuing purpose we have to face situations and things that challenge our every emotion and ultimately our will and commitment to maintain the course.

The truth be told it's far more comfortable for '*an easier life*' to strive for success the way the whole world does, without doing any of that soul-searching stuff. But as we have seen, people are missing vital opportunities to live a fulfilled and purposeful life. Many people who are truly honest will confess that all the accolades of success do not bring fulfilment. They bring convenience, choices and a nice lifestyle, but they don't bring fulfillment, which is the goal. The challenge therefore is to decide whether we're going to pursue our life path of unchartered territory that leads to fulfilment and ultimately makes your soul feel alive? That requires a lifestyle of faith and belief. Or do we settle for an easy relatively predictable life in comfort zones where there's no intrinsic fulfilment but we can try to fit into the world's standards of success if we do all the right things. Ultimately this question is one we have to face in determining whether purpose is something we want to commit to.

Now, there are a lot of self-help books out there, some of which make great reading and contain some really good principles, which more often than not can be located somewhere in the bible. However, as we have already seen in this book, self-help is not the lifestyle that God intended us to live. He created us, has the roadmap of our lives engraved on the palms of His hands and is invested in guiding us to the fulfilment of our lives purpose. Therefore primarily we don't need self-help, we need God's help and divine guidance. As such we must first put in the work to ensure that internally our lives are in alignment with the principles of God. Then very naturally through the growth process discussed, we become aligned with purpose.

I hasten to add that it's not to say that you cannot discover or pursue your passion or gift without God and His Word. Of course it is perfectly possible! However, the fundamental difference is that when your life and soul is surrendered to God and His principles, your talent becomes a vessel that God fills with His Spirit to touch the lives of others in the fulfilment of your purpose. When God isn't at the heart of your soul, your talent can quite easily become a vessel that, if you're not careful, can be filed with ego. Ego is a state of self-absorption where excessive attention to oneself becomes the focus. Purpose however is fulfilled when the mind and soul are rooted in godly principles of serving others with love by the expression of your talent/passions. Purpose has a humble respect for the gift from God that enables one to be used for God's purposes to touch the lives of others. Conversely, the essence of ego is pride-filled where mostly God is an after-thought, if even given any thought at all. With ego the dominating theme and thought is 'self'. Many successful people could attest that at some point in their careers, their egos had to be checked because it took the focus away from their God-given talent and led them down dangerous paths. Ego unchecked leads people into many situations that neither serve the purpose of their soul nor honours the gift that put them onto a platform that enables them to share their gift. God therefore, by the principles of His Word is the anchor that keeps our souls in line and in check whilst we pursue our life path of purpose and fulfilment.

LOVE & PURPOSE: THE INTERLINK

We've seen that as we live in conscious observance and application of God's principles, the expression of our passions in service to the world is absolutely central to the fulfilment of our purpose; The outcome is an expression of love, which is the very essence of God. God is love (1 John 4:8). Fulfilment of our purpose manifests the qualities that are the essence of love, which are the essence of God; patience, kindness, humble, self-controlled, honest, trusting, hopeful and persevering. (1 Corinthians 13:4-8)

How amazing is it to grasp the concept that our very soul came from the Source of Love (God); Our soul has travelled from the spirit realm of eternity, entering this physical realm of time and space on earth, all for the purpose of demonstrating through the unique instrument of our lives using our God-given talents and gifts to do His work in a way that we have been equipped to do in order to manifest the expression of His being and will—that of love (Hebrews 13:21). Within this context it's easier to understand that the purpose for our life is bigger than our career or whatever goal we attach our identity to. The purpose of our lives is to fulfil our destiny.

By this reasoning we can understand how God's Word (the bible) is essentially a guide book of principles on how to live successfully, to manifest through the unique instrument of our lives and talents the spirit and essence of God in spreading love in service to the world.

If we make a relationship with God part of our everyday lifestyle, living in obedience to His Word and enduring all the trials that come along with being a trail-blazing purpose pursuer, there is literally nothing that can stop us from achieving our destiny.

The journey and relationship with God requires us to work daily at mastering the principles of love in our own lives. The point is wonderfully illustrated in the biblical account where one of the teachers of the law asked Jesus which was the greatest commandment (Mark 23:28-31). Jesus responded that it is to love God first and foremost, and then secondly to love each other as ourselves. Jesus said that all the prophets and all the law are summed up in those two commandments. When we honour God (by living in accordance to His Word as the most important and Supreme authority in our lives) we are effectively expressing our love for God and thereby fulfilling the first commandment. By consistently obeying God's Word in our lives causes our mind-sets and behaviours to change and align with his principles of love. The outcome of this is that we *become* an expression of love through our lives, and thereby fulfil the second commandment. Whilst it may all sound incredibly simple, we must not be too hard on ourselves when we sometimes inevitably fall short and make mistakes. We have to remind ourselves that we're limited by our humanity (emotions, will and mind) which we have to constantly strive to align with God's Word of love. This is not always easy, particularly through the myriad of life's challenging situations, and if we're being completely honest, our first response may not necessarily always be one of love.

Having examined the importance of love, it being the essence of God's Word intrinsically linked with our purpose, it becomes quite easy to see how many people sadly live and die without ever experiencing true fulfilment in life. Let's determine to set our foot firmly on the path of our destiny and take faith-filled steps fulfilling our purpose and lasting joy.

THE ORDER OF FULFILMENT

Like everything in life there is a proper order of process and development. This means that as we embark upon our journey of purpose, we must ensure that our own lives are in order; For how can we be ready to serve the things that we haven't yet mastered? Our focus then is to begin to fill ourselves with God -His Word and His love. Our own cup (life) should be so full of love (the presence of God and the Galatians 5 Fruit of the Spirit) that we have the capacity to freely extend love (and it's fruit) to others. The love being referenced here is nothing to do with that which you get from another human. This love is what you get from the endless Source of true love, who is God. When we develop a deep and strong relationship with Him through spending time, reflecting and applying His Word we begin to recognise God moving in our everyday lives.

The love that we get from God is unlike any other in the world. God's love is honest, stable, and unselfish that gives, serves, elevates, empathises and perseveres through all difficulties. We don't develop that embodiment of love within us overnight; It's a life transforming process to become whole and fulfilled in ourselves. As we've already seen, the more we apply it the more we slowly but surely reconfigure our minds and lives to align with God and His Word. In fact, the sooner we get on this journey the better for us as it means that we should be able to navigate our lives out of tricky situations that cause us to go through life searching and depending on things or people to make us feel whole and happy.

GOD FIRST NOT THE OTHER WAY ROUND

When we turn to things or people to try and fulfil us when only God can, it very often leads to into unhealthy and dysfunctional relationships, chronic dependencies and even addictions. Instead of entering relationships in a state of wholeness, we enter them as broken people who have been wounded by life's circumstances and as a result we're needy. We need love, stability and security. When we haven't begun our journey of healing and wholeness we end up situations and relationships where we are not equipped to be able to love another person with a healthy love; Instead our love is rooted in our own neediness and most likely we end up attracted people with the same hurts, wounds and scars as us. Unfortunately, this means that we can mistakenly confuse what with think is love with a relationship of toxic co-dependency and quite often we end up using other people as emotional crutches to help us get through life. This is not how God intended our lives to be. Nothing and no-one but God should be the Source of our strength, joy and fulfilment, and when other people or things become our source, what we are actually doing is creating idols in our lives. We know from God's Word that it is a commandment that we are not to create any idols for ourselves, and therefore this is a serious matter. Throughout His Word, God has been clear that we are to seek *first* His Kingdom and His Ways, and once we consistently do this He is faithful to provide us with all the things that we need (Matthew 6:33). As we've seen, seeking God first means going through the process detailed in this book to know God intimately first; This is through regularly reading and reflecting on His Word, submitting and surrendering to Him, and going through a healing process to become a whole and fulfilled person with a foundation strongly rooted in God.

One of the most important revelations we can ever receive is that LOVE for God and by extension for ourselves is the starting point of all true success and growth in Life. God is life and God is the essence of Love. The more we fill ourselves with God the more we are filled with love , grace, compassion and able to love and give love without ulterior motive or need. The essence of a successful life is to be the personification of love, and is one of the most powerful legacies that we can ever leave in life.

• • •

CHAPTER EIGHT

THE CHANGES WE GO THROUGH

As we go through the transformation process, one of the most significant challenges that we experience is with regard to how our close circle evolves. Not everyone is going to want to commit to the godly transformative path, and even for those that want to, they may not be ready to commit to it at the same pace as us. These situations can present challenges to us, as whilst we're growing and evolving toward a lifestyle of godliness, our circle may not particularly understand the changes that we're going through or even why we have to change so much at all. The more we become centred and focused on God, the more intentional and certain we feel about our identity and purpose in life. This can make the people around us feel uncomfortable, particularly we begin to outgrow the parameters of familiarity. We actually may end up outgrowing certain friendships, or losing the connection that we once had. The key to overcoming such challenges is to recognise and accept that everything is happening for us, and for our good. God allows certain situations to come our way in life to shape, prepare and propel us into the destiny He has prepared for us.

As we grow we may find that we begin to have less things in common than before. We may talk less frequently and find that we are no longer excited about the things we used to talk about. It's possible that our shared interests may wane and generally we outgrow what used to be familiar territory. This part of the process is by no means easy to endure, but it is of course a necessary part of our growth and transformation process. There may even be times that we are faced with a difficult reality of having to accept that certain people and things will not be good for the future and destiny that God has prepared for us. People that are not good for us end up holding us back from moving forward into our destiny. As much as we'd love them to stay, sometimes they are counterproductive to our growth in God and into our destiny. This may mean that we have to let them go if that's the way that God leads.

MORPHING RELATIONSHIPS

This life-long journey into destiny creates not just an evolution within us, but also within our relationships. I've experienced it with my closest girlfriend. We've been friends for over 20 years and are each other's deepest confidants. We have one of those friendships where we often know exactly what the other is thinking just by a single look without the utterance of a word. Yet as close as we are, we are still two very different people and have walked our journey in God at quite difference paces. There were times when we actually wondered whether our friendship would last in the midst of some very challenging moments.

In fact to keep it 100% real there have been times when we just didn't *get* each other, and in our frustrations we've each taken the executive decision to literally *'check out'* of the friendship. At those times we just didn't understand each other and how God was moving in our midst. However as God would have it, no matter how many times we resolved in our minds to break off the friendship, God had distinctly other plans. I've come to realise that some people are in our lives for just a season, whereas others are purposed to stay a few chapters, and some even a lifetime. When God has a plan not even the ignorance of mankind can thwart it. I mean there were literally times that my BFF and I were so stubborn that we refused to contact each other, convinced of our own righteous indignation! However God always found a way to synchronise our paths and bring us back into an even closer relationship than before. Relationships that can stand the test of time, and persevere through trials, especially those with godly foundations are to be deeply treasured for they are most definitely an outstanding gift from God. I can truly say that regardless of any disagreements, my best friend is one of the most important relationships in my life, and I'm sure she feels the same way too. Our individual growth process in God has helped each of us to sharpen each other in mastering the Fruits of the Spirit to equip us with the characteristics to be able to be patient with each other as we figure out our own paths and growth in God. The stronger we grow in God, the more skilful we have become of being the sensitive and empathetic support we've each needed to ensure that any conflict or confusion is kept to a minimum to avoid giving the enemy a foothold in our lives and relationship.

This morphing experience is not true of all my friendships. I've had experiences of friendships with people that I've known for much longer but our life paths were just not aligned for us to grow together. This can often happen when a close friend is so fundamentally opposed to your journey that in order for peace you have to be willing to graciously let go and let God take control of that situation. As a highly reserved introvert person, putting myself out there to befriend people just does not come naturally to me, which means that I deeply cherish my existing friendships. I know the feeling of incessantly hitting roadblocks that seemingly prohibit a natural flow within my relationships. I idealise my friendships and as hard as it sometimes is, I've had to learn to allow some of these friendships to naturally come to an end. These are the painful and graceful moments that force us to consider our own stage of growth and whether we are giving the necessary time and space to others to help them grow as individuals too. Sometimes the issue is that we just don't know how to navigate these difficult issues. There really doesn't need to be any drama or bad feelings when parting ways. All that's required is a peaceful acceptance and surrender to the fact that we're moving into different phases and directions in life without each other. It just means if we reach that phase we have to gracefully let go and allow each other to follow our own path to destiny.

It's easier said than done though and when it comes to letting go of certain relationships it can be extremely difficult. However sooner or later we'll come to realise that if God has been guiding us into letting it go, it really is for our own good. We can insist on doing things our way because God has given us free will to choose our own path, however when we decide to hold onto things that have passed their longevity date in our lives, we'll soon enough learn that holding onto dead things no longer feels good. After a while begin to feel the effects of decomposition; Where the unpleasantness of the situation will literally force us to let go. It's a lesson that many of us will need to learn but God has given us the grace we need to get through those experiences.

THE IMPORTANCE OF LETTING GO: RELATIONSHIPS AND THE PAST

Relationships that reflect the essence of God are pivotal to our destiny walk. We tend to give power to our close relationships to influence our hearts and minds, and thus affects our life perceptions and decisions. Sometimes we'll experience friendships that consistently cause us to compromise with God's Word, or even veer off the course of our destiny. Those friendships are unhelpful in supporting us in walking our life path, and sooner or later we'll need to decide what's more important to us, the friendship or our destiny? These are not easy decisions to make, for we are human! It's normal to wrestle with such decisions, and often the deeper our feelings for the relationship, the greater the struggle to let go. This struggle can show up in any number of ways from not ending a relationship that we know does not honour God/godliness, to constantly dwelling on the past. I hasten to add that this doesn't mean that *all* of our friends have to be Christian, absolutely not! It's important that we have a healthy and diverse range of friendships with all types of people because God requires us to go *'out into the world'* (Mark 16:15) and in the world there's a diverse range of people whom we have to be comfortable engaging with. But when it comes to our *close circle* in whom we confide and allow to speak into our lives, this circle really should reflect our core godly values. The difficulty we experience when we compromise is that we can so very easily be subtly drawn back into a lifestyle that we have been committed to transforming out of, and this can affect our whole walk into destiny.

The other aspect of letting go is the discipline we have to exercise in letting go of people or experiences in our past. There is nothing wrong with looking back from time to time to reflect on our memories in life, and how far we've come but what we must be very careful not to do is have people within our close circle that encourage us to look and gravitate back into our past, or foster deep within us a longing for the life that we left behind in our strive toward leading a life that honours God. By developing feelings of longing for the past leaves our hearts in an extremely vulnerable position of influencing us to return to the past. This is dangerous territory as it literally represents a wall preventing us from growing in our relationship with God and destiny.

We therefore have to be very careful about guarding our hearts against things that would unduly influence us in the wrong way. The bible says our hearts are deceitful above all things (Jeremiah 17:9), and in my experience it has a habit of making us remember the past through rose-tinted glasses. We need to be very careful about how we see and perceive things, because no sooner have we lamented on things of the past, it begins to become deeply embedded within our hearts, growing roots and taking hold over our thoughts, perceptions and decision-making. All of this can be extremely detrimental to us achieving all within our path of destiny.

This was exactly the case in the story of Lot and his wife in Genesis 19. Lot was the nephew of Abraham, who lived with his wife in the city of Sodom. Sodom was a place where the people behaved with great wickedness because their hearts were filled and fixated on evil.

The evil was so bad that the victims' outcry had reached God. He decided that He'd go down and investigate whether the outcry was justified. When God determined that it was indeed justified, He decided to destroy the city of Sodom. But before He did so, God sent His angels to inform Lot of Sodom's fate. The following day as dawn was about to break, the angels urged Lot, his wife and family to leave Sodom. Lot hesitated so much that the angels had to grab his hand and lead him to hurry out of the city. As Lot and his wife were leaving, the angels told them in clear terms to flee for their lives to the mountains, and they must not look back, nor stop anywhere along the journey. Lot was worried about making it to the mountains unharmed and asked the angels if he could stay at a town along the way. His request was granted. His wife however was worried for a different reason; she did not want to leave Sodom as she had a deep emotional attachment to it. As such, along the journey ahead and against the command of the angels, Lot's wife looked back. Yet it wasn't just a look, she looked back with a longing in her heart for the life she was supposed to be leaving behind. Sadly, her desire for the past outweighed the destiny that God's angels were leading her to. In other words she was so deeply emotionally attached to her past that she simply couldn't get over it, and ultimately that very literally led to her destruction; Because she disobeyed the command of God (through His angels) by looking back, demonstrative of her lack of faith she was turned into a pillar of salt. This is a dramatic illustration of what it means to long for situations that God has told us to move on from. It is crucial in our forward movement that we're connected to people that will encourage us to strive toward the destiny of our future.

> 'the godly offer good counsel; they teach right from wrong. They have made God's law their own so they will never slip from his path' —Psalm 37:30

We need to allow God the opportunity to divinely position the right people around us at exactly the right time who can give us godly counsel.

God knows everything we need so trust that He has provided everything we need along our path of life and purpose.

. . .

CHAPTER NINE

NEW IDENTITY NEW POWER

Our new identity emerges all the more clearly the more that we travel through the transformation process submitting our lives to living in obedience to God's Word. The more we do this, the more we mirror the image of God's Word and whom He intended us to become when He created us for life on earth.

God created us with exceptional purpose, for the bible clearly says that we are *wonderfully made*. Although this sounds like a feel good scripture, it actually contains great depth about God's intentionality towards us. In the book of Genesis, as God was creating the world, every *thing* that He spoke into existence, He described as *good;* This included the sun and stars, and the creatures of the earth. God called them all 'good'. However, when it came to the great creatures of the sea, and mankind, God didn't just speak them into existence—He *created* them. This seems to suggest that God paid a great deal more attention to their creation than anything else. Furthermore, when it came to mankind God was even more particular because unlike any of his other creation He gave mankind two distinct features; Mankind was created in own image, and given authority to have power and dominion over the earth. It is in these features that mankind is a special and wonderfully made aspect of God's creation. We have been placed on earth to mirror God's being, power and authority.

We know that Jesus is the Son of God, and that Jesus is God's Word living in human form. He manifested from the spirt realm of eternity and entered the physical realm of earth by being born into mankind. The purpose for this was to restore mankind's direct relationship and direct communication with God. This purpose was achieved when Jesus sacrificed His own life to pay the price for the sins of mankind. Because Jesus paid the ultimate price for mankind's sins, He is the head of all mankind. Jesus was obedient to God the Father through all the human experiences that each of us also go through, even death. He identifies with us when we go through storms and painful experiences because He can empathise with us. Because He paid the price, Jesus is the door through which we enter a relationship with God and accept eternal life. And since God gave Jesus all authority on heaven and earth, Jesus is Lord of all. When we submit ourselves to God's Word (the authority of Jesus) we accept Jesus both as the Lord of our lives, and also our saviour. Our aim should be to live every day in submission to God's Word and in obedience to it.

BACK IN THE DAY: THE FALL

There was an event called the Fall of Mankind, which was when Adam and Eve disobeyed God. The consequence was that mankind became subject to the influence and power of sin. Before the fall, everything on earth was how God created it, good. Man was spiritually alive, alert and in an attuned relationship with God where God and mankind freely conversed. However, in parallel to this Satan existed in the spirit realm. God had cast him out of heaven for disobeying and rebelling against God's authority. Satan's act created sin (the intentional and wilful disobedience to God's Word), and this is the embodiment of Satan's nature.

Satan is a spirit who has a mission, which is to try and usurp God's authority on earth. However he can only manifest his power on earth through using people. Therefore satan will often tempt people to submit to his mission with suggestive thoughts to entice them into doing something that is not aligned with God's Word. When a person succumbs to that thought it gives birth to sin and sin when it is full grown give birth to death (James 1:15).

> *There is a way that seems right to a man, but the end leads to death.* —Proverbs 14:12-13

Therefore the way we are suppose to live is:

> *Trust in **the Lord** with ALL your heart and lean NOT to YOUR OWN UNDERSTANDING. In **ALL** your ways **SUBMIT** to God, and HE will DIRECT your path.*
> —Proverbs 3:5-6

Satan cannot make us do anything, because God has given us free-will. As we have seen, when God created the world He did so with principles to govern every aspect of life. From the changing of seasons to procreation, everything functions good and well when it performs according to the principles that God set. We covered in a previous chapter how God made mankind unique in that He created mankind in His own image which includes the ability to have a will. Trees and the weather don't have a will, but humans do. So our choice is whether we exercise our free-will to submit ourselves to God's principles and mission for life, or whether we will reject God's principles and ways. By not submitting to it, we are rejecting it, which is exactly what satan did and why he got cast out of heaven. Satan's mission is to get us to use our God-given lives to reject God's principles and to do whatever we want in life.

Since we are born spiritually separated from our relationship with God, we can no longer see things from a spiritual perspective with our natural eyes. To obey God we have to follow His Word, which is called walking by faith, because we cannot see in the natural what God has planned in the spiritual because the spiritual realm is unseen to the natural eye. So what satan does is that he creates an illusion in life of how things should be (in disobedience to God), and suggests thoughts to us of how we can make certain outcomes that we want to happen (not God's ways). Satan appeals to our carnal desires, which when our hearts and mind are not submitted to God yield after the things and ways of this world and our fleshly desires. All of this not in adherence to God's principles and Word for life. Therefore, when we are deciding on how to exercise our free-will with our daily life decisions, we are effectively deciding whether we're going to do life God's way or satan's way. There's no in-between. We either follow the principles God laid down in His Word to govern the life that He created, or we reject those principles which is satan's way. To tempt us to follow his way, satan suggests thoughts that make us feel that pride of life of doing things our way according to our own wishes and on our own terms. When a person succumbs to that thought it gives birth to sin.

Unfortunately, when Adam and Eve succumbed to the temptation of Satan, they disobeyed God's Word which resulted in mankind surrendering his God-given power and authority to satan. From that moment, mankind ceased to have direct access in relationship with God, and the world ceased to be 'good' as God had purposed. Mankind had transferred its power and authority over the earth to satan. Satan exercises his power by surrounding the earth with his darkness, hence he is called the price of darkness and he detests the light, which is the presence of God and truth. Satan exercises his power using darkness which is symbolic of the separation of mankind's relationship with God, and therefore leaves mankind unable to understand life according to God's principles. This is why it is vitally important for us to reconnect back into relationship with God, and follow His principles of life in His Word. We follow and obey God's Word by faith, since satan's power of darkness on earth means that we now cannot see or understand God's ways with our natural eyes or mind. With our natural eyes all we see is Satan's power at work trying to discredit to mankind the presence and credibility of God and His Word. Since satan has authority over the earth he manipulates the physical images we see daily to trick our minds to perceive it to be reality. For many of us, seeing is believing as that's the mantra of the culture that we've grown up in, and it also makes us feel good with power and control over our lives (the Pride of Life - 1 John 2:16).

Unlike Adam and Eve before the fall, we can no longer directly converse with God to guide us through life; That is until we make the choice to decide to go though the door which is Jesus to restore our direct relationship with God, as it was intended to be.

Therefore, from the moment that we are born into this earth we are born into a physical realm of darkness which is governed by sin and therefore we are separated from our direct spiritual relationship with God. We know that Jesus came to be door through which we can enter a direct restored relationship with God again. And what about before Jesus came I hear you say?

Well our God is a merciful God who and wanted to redeem our relationship with Him. Therefore before Jesus Christ was born, God spoke to certain people whom He chose to be Prophets and Priests back in the Old Testament. God would speak to them as a means to empower them with His Word to touch people's lives so that they could believe in God and return into relationship with Him to guide them through life.

Our potential and power to fulfil our literal God-given purpose shifts the moment we accept the Word of God as the supreme authority in our lives. At that point we inherit the full capacity to fulfil the powerful and abundant life we have been predestined to achieve. At that moment we become reconnected to the Almighty God, Our Creator who seeks to guide us through along our path of destiny.

NEW PERSPECTIVE: POWER TO ACHIEVE

We must be constantly mindful through our life on earth that the spirit realm is a very real unseen world that exists completely alongside our experiences in this physical world. However often times since we cannot see the spiritual realm with our physical eyes, it is easy for us to forget that it even exists as we go about our daily lives. This again is how satan is able to move so cunningly almost undetected to us in life, unless we are conscious of God's presence around us, and are sensitive in our spirit to know when a contrary spirit is moving in our midst.

As we live in these parallel worlds is critical if we seek to achieve our purpose, for us to constantly nurture our relationship with God and develop our spiritual growth so that God can direct us along our path.

Our spirit loves God but as humans we enjoy the things that satisfy our carnal desires, which are embedded in sin and contrary to God. This is the reason that it is crucially important to master the art of self-control. The extent to which we master self-control determines the extent to which we will exercise our God-given power, and take positive strides to the fulfilment of our destiny.

POWER AND RELATIONSHIP

As Christians we are children of God, and to help us build our relationship with Him God has given us His Holy Spirit to reside within our bodies (which is why our bodies are the temple of God). With the Spirit of Our Father God living inside of us, it's our responsibility to nurture that relationship by communicating with God's Spirit within us. God's Spirit comes alive and empowered when combined with God's Word.

> *many as are led by the Spirit of God are the sons of God.*
> —Romans 8:4

With God's Holy Spirit power within us we have the capacity to achieve everything God created for us in our destiny; The only thing that will stop us from achieving it is our lack of belief in the integrity of God's Word, or our proclivity to give into the temptations of satan which causes us to compromise the integrity of our faith.

To help us understand how God's Word and Spirit guides us in practical life situations, let's take for example that common relationship issue. If we seek God's will for a particular person that we are in a relationship with, and through prayer, peace and scriptural revelation God reveals that this is not the person that He has ordained for us to marry, we have a decision to make. Either we go through the process of separation from that relationship or we remain in it. Sin works like this; If God says no, but we disobey and hold onto the relationship because of our emotional ties or dependency, we are effectively allowing channels of negative decisions and forces to have intimate access to us. These powers of disobedience to God are being manipulated by Satan for the very purpose to prevent us from achieving our God-given destiny. Disobedience is the number one reason why people don't fulfill the plans that God purposed for their lives. One of the key ways satan tries to get us to abort our destiny is to tempt us into getting into and then staying in the wrong relationships, as these do not lead us into fulfilling God's plans.

In the process of this subtle disobedience we truly convince ourselves that we know best and in so doing we compromise God's word because we like doing things that make us feel comfortable in life. We are often so taken by how things appear in this physical realm and comforted by the deceptive paucity of our own dwarfed knowledge against God's wisdom that we indulge ourselves with an abundant amount of grace that we wouldn't dream of extending to others had we been on the outside looking in. That's what pride in self does. What it also does is cause us losses we hadn't foreseen, but for the grace of God. There are many things that we may lose along the way of our own ignorance. At worst we forfeit the fullness of the destiny we have been created to fulfil. We also grant access to the powers of darkness to have control over those aspects of our lives that we have not submitted to God's covering and protection. By slowly separating ourselves from God we subtly destroy our own peace and joy; Sadly we fail to see this immediately as we are blinded by the temporary happiness that we gain through doing this our way instead of God's way. The same way that the power of a life yielded to God's authority can create awesome things, so too the power of a life yielded to Satan's powers and schemes can create terrible stress and discord. It is therefore of primary importance that we trust and adhere to the direction within God's Word which guides us into purposefully fulfilling our purpose in life. By

> *trusting in the Lord with all our hearts and not leaning to our own understanding; in all our ways submitting to Him He will direct our paths* (Proverbs 3:5-7).

When we live a lifestyle where we regularly submit all of our life issues and ways to God, we become perfectly aligned with His power, protection and are empowered to walk into our destiny.

NEW PERSPECTIVE: POWER TO OVERCOME

In addition to having the power to achieve our life's purpose, by having God's Spirit (and therefore power) within us, we have the power to overcome every obstacle and situation that may present itself along the journey of our life path. God says said in His Word that He will not let us be tempted beyond what we can bear. That means that any single situation that God has allowed us to go *through,* He already knows that He has given us everything we could possibly need to get through it. The problem that many of us find is that when we are going through situations, instead of us focussing our minds and energy on God we end up almost entirely focussed on the problem, which discourages us and depletes our power and joy.

God also says that when we are faced with a tempting situation, we should be assured that He has already provided a way of escape so that we may be able to bear and overcome the temptation. Again, this means that God honours His Word when He says that He has gone before us to prepare the way that we should take. If we focus our minds and energy on Him, He will most definitely direct us along the right path. This is a very clear illustration that walking a life submitted to God is not one that is plain sailing free of trials and tribulations. We come to realise that just as we go to the gym to work our physical muscles and endure the pain of a full-on workout, God puts us through the faith gym to work our spiritual muscles to build our faith. He knows exactly what we can take and He won't put a weight on our bar any heavier than we can bear; Yes we will be challenged but no we will not be taken out as long as we keep our focus on God. No season, however good or bad it is lasts for ever, for God said of life principles that:

> *"While the earth remains, Seedtime and harvest, cold and heat, winter and summer, Andy day and night shall not cease."*
> —Genesis 8:22

Seasons dominate the order and flow of life. As such we need to accept that whilst there will be seasons of greatness, that season will change for a while to allow tests and temptation all designed to build our faith and relationship with God as we learn to know and trust Him even more deeply. Accepting this may not be easy but we have to know that whatever season we find ourselves in, we can be assured that God knows our exact circumstances, and whether we understand these perplexing seasons or not, we would be wise to know that God has allowed those seasons of trial to enter our lives as opportunities and experience that are catalysts to our growth in Him. These are just storms, which are known by different names such as 'tests', 'trials', 'temptations', 'mountains' and even 'the evil day'. One thing is for sure, these storms are blessings inside out and at some point in the future we will be able to look back in retrospect and see how seasons of seeming disappointment were spectacularly crafted by the magnificent hand of God to bring us into a deeper and more revelatory experience of knowing and growing deeper in our relationship with Him. We must remember that God's thoughts and His ways are higher than ours (Isaiah 55:9) and so whilst in the 'heights' of our understanding things may look disappointing, God sees things in His omniscient knowledge that every situation in our life is working for our good—it is us who has to adjust our focus, trust and belief.

Even when we look at the Lord's Prayer, it is clear even there that the season of trial or temptation has been permitted by God to come our way:

Lead us not into temptation [please God do not allow us to be tempted or face trials of our faith and faithfulness to you]

But deliver us from evil [Our first request is that you do not allow us to be tempted, but if it is your will for us to be tried, tested and tempted, please Lord deliver us from being overcome by evil]. —Matthew 6:13

. . .

CHAPTER TEN

TRIALS, TESTS & TEMPTATIONS

"Put on the full armour of God, so that when the day of evil comes, you may be able to stand your ground, and after you have done everything, to stand."

EPHESIANS 6:13

We've clearly examined that the simple fact is that life consists of season that will change, sometimes for what we like, and others for what we would rather skip. Therefore it is supremely important that we are firmly rooted in a deep and personal relationship with God and His Word for ourselves so that whatever season we find ourselves in, especially if it is a stormy one that seeks to challenge us to the very core, we can remain firmly planted in the truth of God's Word.

THE PURPOSE OF TRIALS

God never allows trials to come our way to destroy us, and in fact quite the opposite. God is our Father and Maker who intricately knows each of us very well. God knows that we like comfort zones, but He is not in the business of stagnation in comfort zones. He has created our lives with purpose, which means that through each stage of our lives there will be circumstances and situations that we will face which have been ordained by God to pull out, sharpen, refine, teach and equip us with all the virtues and character that we need to be ready for His use.

In a nutshell, trials are part of the process we have to endure as they are the catalysts of our own growth to enable us to go through and be prepared and refined for God's glory to shine through our lives. In order to be faithful stewards of the destiny that God has created for us, we need to get rid of our preconceptions. This means that God has to purge us of our old unrighteous ways and mindsets in order to build us up internally and spiritually in His way of righteousness, love, patience and grace.

Even with the best will in the world, these are not virtues that can be learned overnight, but are borne out of experiences as we travel through life. Sometimes we may not learn the lesson the first time, or even the second time and that's fine with God. Even in our weaknesses and failures He still loves us; In fact especially in these times because when we humbly accept our shortcomings we are perfectly poised to seek His grace. God's grace is sufficient for us because His Word says that His strength is perfected in our weaknesses (2 Corinthians 12:7). That doesn't mean that if we accept we're weak that God will give us a free pass! Oh no, we have to learn that lesson He's trying to teach us and every time we don't complete it, God is faithful to keep us going round (and around) the mountain of experience until we heed that lesson. In life we do not qualify to graduate to the next level of growth and our relationship with God until we pass the test of our current level. This is exactly what God done with the children of Israel when He led them out of bondage in Egypt.

However, just like the Children of Israel, God will not permit us to inhabit the reward and land of promise whilst we are living a lifestyle in rebellion and unsubmitted to His Word. What type of father rewards a rebellious child? The reward will accelerate the child's destruction! Thus in order to purge the Children of Israel from their old ways doing things '*their way*' (where they worshipped false gods instead of the One True God) God had to take them through a myriad of experiences to teach them that He is their faithful God—their Provider, their Protector, their Righteous Judge who has good plans for their lives. Those people that truly learned this lesson entered the Land of Promise. God takes us on the same spiritual journey through life, except our destination is eternal.

There was much for the Children of Israel to learn, particularly in the context that for generations they had been living a life devoid of any reverence or acknowledgement of God. As such God took them on a life journey to purge them of their old way of thinking, and teach them how to live life according to His principles in submission to Him. Along the journey of their new life path, they encountered a number of trials which were ordained by God for a number of reasons:

1. To teach them who He is and His ways so that they'd live in full obedience to Him, and thereby abandon their old ways and false worship as they had done in Egypt.

2. To build a relationship of trust and confidence with them on full reliance of His Word to guide them along the path of their new life.

3. Reliance on Him alone as their one and only God.

The journey to the Promised Land should have only taken them a mere 11-days. However because of their disobedience they had much to learn before God could allow them to possess the Promised Land. The journey of lessons took a whole 40 years. Why so long? Because they had to unlearn habits, mindsets, generational ways in order to develop their relationship with God and submit their lives to Him.

There were many times during the journey that they acted in defiance and rebellion, or failed to trust Him; Many times that they doubted the faithfulness of God's Word and outside of their comfort zones longed to go back to bondage in Egypt. Lack of their faith and belief in God in these situations added to the time that they had to travel around the mountain to develop their trust in God. This is the same experience that we each have today in our own individual life journey with God. Just like the Children of Israel, God has a Promise for us which is the destiny that He created for our souls to fulfil in life. However in order for us to inhabit that destiny, we have to travel along the journey of various trials much like the Children of Israel to teach us about God, and develop our relationship with Him. The trials that the Children of Israel encountered largely involved trusting God to provide their daily basic needs like food. This is what is referred to as *'our daily bread'* in the Lord's Prayer. God gave the Children of Israel His Word that He would provide their needs. He faithfully did so by daily providing manna (bread) as their daily sustenance (Exodus 16). This was to clearly reveal to them that He is their consistent Provider. When Pharaoh's enemies came against them, God parted the Red Sea for them to pass through, and when their enemies pursued, God protected them by closing the waters and drowning their enemies—This was God revealing to them that He was their Protector. These are all lessons and principles that God has established to govern life, and once we understand these principles, our job is to apply them to our lives. This is wisdom; The successful application of biblical principles to our lives.

Another important principle that God wanted them to understand was the fundamental need to respect the people that He had put in positions of authority. God appointed Moses to lead them along the journey. When Moses's sister Miriam began to talk against him behind his back with the intention to usurp his God-given authority, God intervened and revealed to her that He is the righteous Judge of hidden motives deep within the heart of man. God showed this by inflicting a defiling skin disease which turned her skin white for the sins of challenging godly authority. This skin condition in the community meant that she had to be confined outside of the camp. God caused the Children of Israel to travel through a myriad of experiences and circumstances, but not to hurt or harm them; To reveal to them His character, principles and essence so that they could know and have a deep and meaningful relationship with Him as their God, and them as His people through life.

Although these days we don't live the nomadic lifestyle of ancient biblical times, we have our own seasons of trials and proverbial experiences of walking around mountains in the wilderness. Although the landscape of time is different, God uses circumstances in our lives in much the same way to teach us about Him, reveal His character to us so that we can move closer to the fulfilment of our destiny. It is of great assurance to know that God has literally given us His Word that no matter how hard these trials get, they definitely won't last forever. As such we can be confident that we will not tested beyond what we are able to bear. This clearly shows us that God, contrary to widespread belief, is not primarily a punitive God. He longs to share a relationship with us, to guide us into the good plans that He carefully prepared within our destiny. Our job is to transcend the experience of living a physical life on earth to become more conscious and intentional of the true essence of our being—living spiritual souls having an experience in a physical realm for the purpose of fulfilling a life plan (destiny) meticulously designed by God each day of our lives.

It is important to have an understanding of the strategy that God's Word says will provide us with the ability to successfully endure the trials. It is likened to going to war, and thus being prepared and equipped is a critical part of winning that war.

> *Therefore take up the whole armour of God that you may be able to withstand in the evil day, and having done all, to stand.*
>
> *Stand therefore, having girded your waist with **truth**, having put on the breastplate of **righteousness**, and having shod your feet with the preparation of the **gospel of peace**; above all, taking the shield of **faith** with which you will be able to quench all the fiery darts of the wicked one. And take the helmet of **salvation**, and the sword of the **Spirit**, which is the **word of God**; praying always with all prayer*

*and supplication in the Spirit, **being watchful** to this end with all **perseverance** and supplication for all the saints.*
—Ephesians 6

We need to have our whole character, mind, heart and soul equipped and protected if we are to successfully withstand and emerge triumphantly from these tests and trials.

POSTURE TO SUCCEED THROUGH TRIALS

It means that whatever situation we find ourselves in, we must do the following;

1. Remember who we are in Christ—that we are covered and protected by His authority when we submit and commit our life decisions under the authority of God's Word;

2. We must behave in the righteousness and love of God;

3. Conduct ourselves peacefully;

4. Stand firm despite the circumstances in faith on God's Word;

5. Be attentive and yielded to the power of God working through His Holy Spirit guiding us within our situations.

Knowing and understanding the Word of God for ourselves helps us to discern very clearly when the enemy tries to confuse us in the midst of our trials. When we know our God and His Word we can easily identify the enemy's lies using the filter of truth, God's Word. As such our lifestyles should portray to the world a God-consciousness where we have at the forefront of our minds and deeply embedded within our heart and character God's principles for living.

A MICROSCOPIC LOOK AT TRIALS

It's all very well knowing that we will be tested, however it is a very different matter when we're actually going through a trial. At these times God usually goes quiet and we may begin to question so many things—*'is this storm a punishment' 'Did God really say?' 'Surely if I was doing God's will life wouldn't be this hard', 'this trial is lasting too long, I must have heard God incorrectly'; 'God's way isn't working so now I have to do things my own way'.* These are very real thoughts that come to us to try and take us off the course to our destiny, and often times we can legitimise in our own wisdom why we should take the wheel instead of allowing our faith to navigate it for us. For us to endure through such challenging times it is important for us to have two fundamental things; (i). an understanding of God's Word, and (ii). an understanding of the process of growth in God.

UNDERSTANDING GOD'S WORD: DEVELOPING RELATIONSHIP

As has been mentioned before, walking in the destiny that God has prepared for us takes much more than just a superficial level acquaintance with His Word. God *is* His Word and in order for us to have a deep and meaningful relationship with Him, we need to have an insightful understanding of His Word. Once we understand His Word, God will give us the wisdom to know how His Word applies to our own individual life situations into His will. It is important to understand at this point that the bible is a book of *principles for life*. A principle is a fundamental truth that serves as the foundation of something. Therefore if we fully understand that God's Word (the bible) sets out principles that God established to govern and set the foundations for life it equips us to walk with more ease and enlightenment the path of our lives in the fulfilment of our God-given destiny.

Understanding God's Word in a personal way for our own lives develops a very strong bond in our relationship with Him. This is absolutely crucial during times of trial, which we know fundamentally come to test and try the depth of our relationship with God and our trust in Him. It's a basic truth that if we're facing a difficult trial and we don't have a proper understanding of God's Word and trust Him, it is highly unlikely that we're going to be able to fully trust Him to rely on Him to lead us into answers to resolve our trials. All we will see is our dire situation with no way out. This can give rise to a compelling need to act in our own strength and wisdom. In the life of Job we get a great example of how we are suppose to handle trials.

JOB'S LIFE: THE PERFECT EXAMPLE WHEN FACING TRIALS

Job is a man who had obviously taken the time to develop his relationship with God by acquainting himself with God's Word. The bible says Job 'knew' and 'feared' (revered) God and avoided engaging in any kind of wrongdoing.

There was a particular day when satan presented himself to God to explain what he was doing. Satan said that he was going back and forth on the earth, and the reason why is explained in 1 Peter 5:8—we are told to *be alert and in control of our minds* because the devil, our enemy is prowling round like a roaring lion looking for someone to devour. Lions roar when they are announcing their territory, a place that they can rule. So when satan tells God that he was going back and forth on the earth, what he was actually doing was intensely searching for someone whose life and destiny he could gain control over, claim as his territory, and ultimately all with the purpose to destroy God's plan and destiny for that life.

Let's just pause here to gather our thoughts and consider what we 'think' should happen next. Most people would say that because Job is faithful, God would protect Job as a blessing for committing and submitting his life to God. That is an extremely sensible response, but that is not what actually happened. God, knowing how strong Job's bond with Him was, and Job's loyalty to His Word, asked satan *"have you considered my servant Job, There is no one on earth like him; he is blameless and upright, a man who fears God and shuns evil?".* God wasn't hiding Job from satan's plan to seek someone to destroy, quite the opposite. God was bolding presenting His crème de la crème of servants of mankind, Job. Why did God do this? Because God knows what our strengths, our weaknesses, how we are going to react in given situations and knows at what point we will turn to Him to seek out His strength to guide us and perfect us in our moments of great weakness (2 Corinthians 12:7-10).

In short God was so confident in Job's ability to withstand satan's tests that He brought Job out for satan to consider. Without a doubt the book of Job is most definitely one to thoroughly study, but in short what happens is that God removed His hedge of protection from around Job's life. As a result Job's life was exposed, and not only that, God granted satan permission to touch and test Job. This is how eager satan is to destroy God's people; As soon as God removed the hedge of protection, satan went out and destroyed Job's livelihood. All of his livestock were stolen and killed, along with all of his servants except the one who had returned to Job to report what had happened.

Straight after that Job's seven sons and three daughters were killed. At hearing all this terrible news Job fell to the ground in worship and not once did he blame God for any wrongdoing to him. After satan saw that Job remained faithful to God satan went back and asked God if he could strike Job's health. God granted this wish with the restriction that satan could not touch Job's life. Again with great immediacy Satan went back to Job and inflicted him with painful sores from the crown of his head to the soles of his feet.

This was unquestionably a major trial of Job's faithfulness to God. It's not clear how long Job's trial lasted, although it was more than a week long. Through it all not once did Job sin by blaming God for his perils. This is remarkable because even when his wife and close three friends who sat with him in the trial spoke against God, Job maintained his loyalty to God.

Sometimes when we are going through trials of our faith in life it feels like everything is falling apart, and like Job's trials in the midst of all the seeming chaos God is silent. It's extremely tempting for us when we don't understand what's happening in our lives to try and rationalise things in our own understanding. But one of the things that we can learn from Job's experience is that even our closest loved ones cannot be relied upon to get us through some trials of our faith. The only way we can get the strength and maintain soundness of mind through our trials is to remain faithful to God and His Word, as Job did. This means that no matter what is happening to or around us, we choose not to focus our minds on it, but instead we steadfastly focus, mediate and increase our belief in the integrity of God's Word—that God is good and that His plans (although we don't understand this bewildering season) are for our good and not for evil. Many of us when we're in the midst of trials behave as Job's wife and friends did; we start speaking out of our fear of the circumstances and speak foolishly against God. It's clear to see from Job's trial that this is not the way that pleases God. Job is our example. God is faithful and the seasons will absolutely change, but we just have to endure them with patience and focus our focus and attention on God, regardless of what we see with our physical eyes and what we can or cannot understand.

Finally one day God spoke to Job out of the storm and trials. God explained to Job the vast magnitude of His power and authority over the whole universe. He did this to illustrate to Job that whatever is going on in his life is not outside the reach and knowledge and power of God. After God had spoken, Job realised that despite his closeness to God, there were still some aspects to God that even he hadn't fully appreciated about God's omnipotence, omnipresence and omniscience.

God was angry with Job's friends for their conduct during Job's trial, and told Job that he had to pray for them. After he did this, God restored Job's fortunes and rewarded him for his faithfulness through the trial. Do you know how God rewarded Job? For everything that Job lost, God gave him back double! He blessed the latter part of Job's life far greater than the former part of it. I think it's safe to say that this trial was probably the most defining moment of Job's life. Job was one person before 'that trial' and completely someone else after it. He had endured a monumental test. I suspect that when Job took some meditative time out and reflected back on that period in his life, it probably left him completely astounded to know that even when it looked as if all hell was breaking loose around Him, and not a spoken Word from God, that God was actually with him the whole entire time. God had Job's entire life path mapped out and part of His plan was to deliberately allow Job to go through that experience in order to bring Job into a deeper knowledge and closer relationship with God. And not only that but for those in Job's life to witness the immense power of God and not to limit what God can or cannot do.

This is actually a very important lesson, as oftentimes in our trials, those well-meaning people in our close circle will impress upon us their opinions on what we should and shouldn't do. What we can clearly see is that every man must know God deeply for himself. Job knew God and knew not to charge God with any wrongdoing. However the same could not be said of the people in Job's close circle. There can be some people in our close circle that seem very religious and that perhaps have even going to church without fail their whole lives. Being religious and regular church attendance, even years of consistently doing various acts of service in the church is not the same as knowing God. Knowing God means that we've spent time reading His Word, speaking to God about how His Word applies to our lives, we've sat in quiet meditation reflecting on the thoughts we have in those holy moments and we've committed to doing our utmost best at applying God's Word to our lives. Church attendance and appearing pious has nothing to do with any of this. Developing our relationship with God is a personal lifestyle commitment that happens profoundly in the heart of man. Therefore, since nobody but God and the spirit within a man knows the heart of a man, we have to be able to know God for ourselves and let the conviction of God's Word and Spirit within us be our guide to navigate and strengthen us in trials (1 Corinthians 2:11).

One of the most confusing things I ever heard as a newly saved Christian was that *everything I need is already provided for in God's Word*, it made absolutely no sense to me. However with time I came to understand that the bible is a book of principles, and I understood that when facing a dilemma all I need to do is prayerfully ask God for wisdom in knowing how to apply His principles to my own daily life. The first step toward acquiring this wisdom is by studying God's Word, the bible. Some people may find this easier either alone or as part of a study group. It really doesn't matter how a person starts off, but what is important is that we make it a lifestyle habit to study to get a very good understanding of the principles that God has laid out throughout His Word. I would even go as far to say that it is imperative even after a group bible study to have some alone time with God to prayerfully reflect on what we've learned about His Word and to ask God for wisdom on how that knowledge would apply to our everyday life. In short, wisdom is the successful application of biblical knowledge to life. There is something to learn in every part of God's Word for our own lives, either for our present situations, those to come or even to equip us with godly wisdom to be a blessing to someone else who may be going through a challenging time who needs a word of encouragement. If we take the time to study and acquire biblical knowledge of the principles then God by His Spirit will guide our thoughts with the strategy on how to successfully apply our His principles to our life situations.

CHAPTER ELEVEN

THE GROWTH PROCESS

UNDERSTANDING GROWTH IN GOD

As we've been able to see, growing in God is a steady process that happens over time according to the amount of time and commitment we invest in our relationship with God. Our mind-sets, perspective and behaviours steadily change which develops our knowledge of God's Word and thus developing our relationship with Him. The more we apply it to our lives, the more we gain revelation and understanding of God and His direction for our lives.

The process of growing in God is even reflected in nature around us, for it mirrors His principles for growth and life. In fact the bible clearly says that God's creation speaks of Him:

> "Ever since the creation of the world his eternal power and divine nature, invisible though they are, have been understood and seen through the things He has made. So they are without excuse." —Romans 1:20

> "Ask the animals, and they will teach you, or the birds of the air, and they will tell you; or speak to the earth, and it will teach you, or let the fish of the sea inform you. Which of these does not know that the hand of the Lord has done this? In His hand is the life of every creature and the breath of all mankind." —Job 12:7-10

> "Praise the Lord from the earth, you great sea creatures and all ocean depths, lightning and hail, snow and clouds, stormy winds that do His bidding, you mountains and all hills, fruit trees and all cedars, wild animals and all cattle, small creatures and flying birds." —Psalm 148:7-10

It is clear to see from these scriptures that when each of God's creation functions according to how He designed and purposed them, by their very existence they each testify of God's glory and magnificence. The same principle applies to each of us; God has created us in His image to walk the course of our life path and fulfil the purposes that He designed for us. In doing so, in a life surrendered and obedient to His Word, just like nature that surrounds us we will also testify to the world God's glory and presence.

> For we are God's masterpiece. He has created us anew in Christ Jesus, so we can do the good things He planned for us long ago. —Ephesians 2:10

It is very clear from this scripture that we have been created for specific and special purposes chosen by God. Thus in order to successfully live the purpose that God has created for us, we must first seek God in order to know Him, and by knowing Him He guides us along the path of our destiny to fulfil our purpose. It's all a process, and just as stated above, we can even witness the process in considering by analogy the basic process of plant growth. This is actually an important illustration because God Himself stated that seedtime and harvest time are one of the governing principles for life, a life He expects us to be fruitful in.

Therefore we start at the beginning of the process, principally bearing in mind that we are at our core, souls that have emanated from the spirit realm, and we've now arrived on earth to have as a soul a human experience on earth. We remain souls throughout this process, and the growth we are going through is a spiritual growth of our soul within a human body that exists in a physical realm.

For us to achieve our destiny our souls need to grow. Our souls are akin to seeds which we need to nurture and care for, illustrated by the process below.

GROWING INTO DESTINY: AN ILLUSTRATION

Stage 1—Preparation: Firstly it is necessary to prepare the soil to ensure that the environment is optimal to enable the seeds to develop into their full potential. This is exactly what God did in the creation of the earth (Genesis 2). Before God made mankind, He prepared the earth and put the seeds in their place. However, God didn't send rain, or cause any shrub to appear until He made mankind to tend to it. (lesson: when God places you in an environment, He already knows what you need and has strategically placed the right people and resources around you in order to nurture your growth process).

As soon as God had finished forming Adam and creating Eve, He made all the trees grow out of the ground. Each one of us are God's (soul) seeds in this world and realm. When we have surrendered our lives to Christ, God puts us through the growth process, which starts off with this first stage by putting us in an environment that will give us the optimal experiences to promote and nurture our growth.

Stage 2—Planting: The next stage is planting the seeds underground. When we go through this stage of our spiritual growth it may seem as if life is literally falling apart. We surrender to God and then all of a sudden we're surrounded by chaotic situations. This can feel baffling as it's a common misconception that a life surrendered to God is meant to be free from significant challenges. The planting stage is about developing our walk of faith; We'll be presented with situations that with our natural eyes and understanding looks entirely hopeless. However, the our eyes and understanding are covered by the darkness of this world, and the only thing that will get us through is trusting and depending on God through the darkness with the eye of faith in His Word. We begin to understand that God doesn't want us to have full control of our lives, but rather for us to depend on Him to guide us along the life path that He predestined for us. This stage feels deeply uncomfortable, and it's not uncommon to feel as if we're buried in troubles. As scary as it may feel God's Word repeatedly tells us to fear not, because it's all part of the process. We have not been buried, we have been planted. It's vital in times of trial that we remember this. During this time, the enemy, like in the book of Job will tempt us into thinking that God has forgotten about us, and that whatever situation we're facing is entirely hopeless and that we need to save ourselves using the strategies satan suggests as he tries to infiltrate our thoughts. We must not allow the illusion of what life 'appears' to be take us off our spiritual growth path and loyalty to God.

Stage 3—Growth under the ground: This stage is succinctly explained by the following quote:

> *"For a seed to achieve its greatest expression, it must come completely undone. The shell cracks, its insides come out and everything changes. To someone who doesn't understand growth, it would look like complete destruction".* —Cynthia Occelli

The greatest expression of our lives is when we become whom God predestined us. However in order to do achieve this stage where we are the greatest expression, it is imperative and unavoidable for us to go through a process of 'unbecoming'. This requires us to release from the world's ways of doing things and re-program our minds to think according to God's principles and ways. We replace our old way of thinking with the principles of God's Word to help us renew our minds. We therefore water the seeds of our lives with the water of God's Word to empower us to grow according to His principles for life. In reality onlookers may look at our lives and to them it may appear that our life is cracking and falling apart. But we're not cracking, we're growing in God.

Stage 4—Germination: At this stage a seedling bursts out of the shell, and it must be exposed to light to enable it to grow strong. The seedling must therefore push up against gravity through the earth's dirt for it to appear in the next level and dimension of its growth above ground. This is exactly what we go through. When it seems as if we're buried in challenges, God gives us strength to push through past them into the next dimension of our growth and destiny. We gain that strength using the light of God's Word, which encourages, guides, empowers and comforts us as we move along the path of our growth toward the fulfilment of our life's purpose.

> *Your Word is a lamp to my feet and a light to my path*
> —Psalm 119:105

Stage 5—Movement and separation: Once a seedling begins to bear leaves, it is a sign that it is necessary for the plant to be moved away from the rest of the seedlings into its own individual pot. When we have gone through an exponential season of challenges and growth in God, oftentimes like Job we go through these seasons in our own lives but the people around us haven't experienced growth quite at the same level. Job's friends didn't understand it and spoke against God. Even's Job's wife thought that he had sinned. None of them realised that every rough situation Job had faced was carefully planned by God to be the catalyst in the development of Job's faith and relationship further with God. Because God is so invested in us watching us develop and outgrow our current environment, it becomes necessary for us to become separated from certain people in our environment. We must remember our nearest and dearest people may not be so discerning and may actually fall for Satan's own strategies. Therefore it's imperative that we find a quiet space where we can pray and reflect on God, His Word and await to hear Him clearly, so that His voice is not be drowned out by the opinions of those closely connected to us. In our place of solitude it's easier to study and meditate on God's Word and it is a necessary part of our growth. When the seedling has been moved into its own pot it has to be taken care of to enable its roots to grow into the new compost. In the same way, when God moves us to the next level of our destiny, He guards and takes care of us to enable us to adapt to our new environment. This helps us to develop even stronger roots in our relationship with Him.

Stage 6—Further change of environment: The seedling can only remain in its own individual pot for a certain amount of time. After a while it grows into a plant and outgrows its singular pot environment. One of the signs that the seedling has outgrown its environment is that the roots start to emerge from the bottom of the pot. At this point further change is necessary to enable it to be planted out in its final location for expansive growth. In our own spiritual development, once we have gone through the soul-wrenching transformative process of spiritual growth, we are ready to be planted in the precise place that God predestined and prepared for us to bear fruit. Just like the seedling, we will have outgrown our former environments because our roots and relationship with God will have deepened so significantly that we could not remain in those past environments and still fulfil the highest expression that God has predestined us to become. Like the seedling, in order for us to achieve our highest expression, we will need to move to an environment that is conducive to the expansion of our growth and development into the great destiny God has prepared for us. Achieving this stage is the pinnacle of our spiritual growth, for reaching this stage means that we have been able to transform our identity from our former ways into the image that God destined us to become, and in the process mirroring His character, love and Spirit. It is that most challenging transformation journey that qualifies us to inhabit and shine in that expansive space, fulfilling our purpose and emanating the glory of God.

Typically at this stage in our growth process, we will be using our God-given passions, gifts and talents to serve in the world. This can be anything from being an artist to being a teacher, but whatever we are doing, the spirit of God's love and excellence will emanate from our being. Further, as we continue to serve faithfully represent God well with diligence and excellence, He provides us with a sphere of influence amongst people with whom we have a natural synergy. Using our God-given talents and gifts, we will naturally encourage and empower people to travel their own life path at whatever intersection we've met them at. And if we're serving God right, people will be able to tell that there is something positive that sets us apart from the crowd, and draws people to us and enables us to connect with our purpose. This stage is about being fruitful with our lives (Galatians 5:22 and Philippians 2:14) and being sure that when this life is over, God will be pleased with the ways that put our lives to work for His glory, just as in the Parable of Talents (Matthew 25: 14-30).

This overview is a very simplified analogy of the process of our godly spiritual growth. Simple as it may be, it serves as an illustration to help us identify the stage that we may be at, and to serve as encouragement that in life everything is subject to change with the seasons we're in. We cannot get caught up and emotionally too attached to any particular season that we're in, particularly if it's a season of comfort zones. Our growth and purpose require us to travel though the seasons of change. Whether we find ourselves in the midst of trials, or a season of relative calm, we can rest assured that whatever the season, God has permitted it to fulfil His divine plan for our good, and to usher us deeper into relationship with Him and purpose.

In life, we know good fruit when we see and taste it. In terms of our spiritual journey, good fruit is characterised by developing our relationship with God, enduring the tests of our faith, and developing godly character from seed-form, in order to refine us into the person that God has predestined us to become and live the destiny that we've been created to fulfil.

∴

CHAPTER TWELVE

LIVING YOUR DESTINY

"If you had any idea whom you're destined to become and the impact your life will have, it would literally blow you away".

It has been said that the graveyard is the richest place on earth, because it is there that we will find all the hopes and dreams that were never fulfilled; The books that were never written, the songs that were never sung, the inventions that were never shared and the cures that were never discovered. Why? All because someone was too afraid to take that first step, keep with the problem or was not determined enough to persevere with their dream.

There are literally millions of people who have died without fulfilling the greatness for which they were created—the thought of stepping out onto unknown paths and unchartered waters cripples people with fear. Or perhaps it's the feeling of personal inadequacies that inhibit people from believing that they possess the God-given capacity to achieve greatness. It is likely that some people live in oblivion of the magnitude of the spirit realm and the ability to connect with God. By not re-establishing our relationship with God on earth, we travel through life like everyone else in the world. This means adopting the world's culture and ways of doing things, and defining our lives and plans according to what we will, not what God wills. This whole book has taken us step by step to illustrate that following the world's ways leaves us unfulfilled, but God's ways direct our paths along the course of our destiny to become the person God pre-destined and fulfil our purpose with the plans, gifts and talents that He has given to us.

The end goal is not just to identify your talent, but also to use your God-given talents for its intended purpose. With God that purpose is always one of service to Him and others..

Fundamentally, that's the purpose of this book—to draw every reader into a closer more intimate relationship with God; To arouse the passion to get to know Him in a more profoundly deeper way, and through time and process become prepared and equipped to live the destiny that God has prepared for us. I can think of nothing more satisfying and rewarding in life than to use one's own unique passions and talents as a vessel through which people can feel, see and experience the graceful, empowering, comforting unconditional love of God.

To submit to God is a double blessing because we get to live a fulfilling and thoroughly enjoyable life doing what we love, and at the same time we live a life that's pleasing and honourable to God using our passions, talents and gifts in service back to Him, and to people in the world around us. This is the hallmark of a life truly well-lived!

There are some remarkable and amazing people who used their passions and love for God to touch the world and leave an indelible mark in history. People such as Mother Teresa who had a passion for people, and dedicated her life to caring for the destitute and dying in the slums of Kolkata. She founded a charity to look after abandoned babies and to help the poorest of the poor, once saying that they "*lived like animals but die like angels*". Consider also Dr Martin Luther King Jr, a Baptist Minister who was passionate about God and loved people, who dedicated his life to seeking equality, civil rights and equal treatment for some of the most oppressed, marginalised and disenfranchised people in American society. The efforts he invested throughout his life made a significant contribution to the advancement of civil rights for African Americans in the United States of America. Who knows the impact that your life may have on this world! It is not necessary to have to have the popularity of Mother Teresa or Dr Martin Luther King Jr, but certainly one of the greatest hallmarks of succeeding in life is seen by using your life as a vessel through which people come to know and recognise the love and presence of God. Quite simply to have left this world in some way better for having lived within it.

A SPECIAL DESTINY AWAITS

As extraordinary as these people have been, there is actually nothing that makes them more or less special than any of us. We *all* have the capacity within us to use our talents, gifts and passions to pursue our dreams and fulfil our noble God-given path designed for us to be a blessing to the world. However, whether we will choose to take the path of faith is entirely up to us. We've seen that the path of faith will seem to our human intelligence very uncertain, even risky and will definitely require us to leave our comfort zones. We've seen that there are countless examples in the bible of God calling people out of ordinary situations in order to prepare them to do extraordinary quests with their life on earth. That first step like Abraham will require us to leave our comfort zones and things familiar to us (Genesis 12:1). Like Moses it will stretch us to follow by faith the path that God is directing us along in fulfillment of our destiny (Exodus 4:1-16). It may even be that we find ourselves in what seems an uncertain situation and the only path out seems scary, but that may be the path that God is beckoning us to take like Peter(Matthew 22-33). What God's Word repeatedly illustrates is that He is faithful. If God leads us onto a certain path, we are more than able to travel along it because He has already equipped us and prepared the way before us.

The issue therefore is not whether God will be faithful; It is whether our knowledge, relationship, belief and trust in Him is developed enough to enable us to surrender complete trust and control to Him. Is our belief in God strong enough that we can rest on that belief to trust in God that no matter what we face, whether it is a storm like Job, or a promise like Abraham, we can trust God as He leads us along our life path to fulfil our dreams, purpose and calling. We have been given this one life by God with a finite number of days, minutes, hours and seconds. How we choose to invest our days, whether to do what we want, or to follow the path that He created us to fulfil, is entirely up to us.

THE FIRST STEP

We have seen throughout the course of this book that God loves each one of us and has taken great care to design a path of destiny in order for us to make a difference in the world with our lives. God invested so much that He didn't want us to remain eternally separated from Him (the consequence of Adam and Eve disobeying God). Therefore God has given us the opportunity to restore our relationship with Him. All we have to do is believe that His Word is true, and that Jesus Christ is God's living Word who paid the price of sin which is death and eternal separation so that we don't have to. If we accept Jesus Christ as the Lord of our lives, to guide and direct our life path, then we are taking that phenomenal step to walking in fulfilment of our life's purpose.

After that, as we've seen, all we need to do is follow the principles for life which are provided within God's Word; It contains all the principles we need to direct us in life into the fulfilment of our God-given destiny.

BLESSINGS FOR OBEDIENCE

God explains in His Word the blessings that He has prepared for us as we obey His Word, in Deuteronomy 28. It definitely is a must read, as it clearly shows that living for God is a win-win life investment. God has also been equally clear about the consequences for refusing to live according to His principles governing life:

> *Now what I am commanding you today is not too difficult for you or beyond your reach. It is not up in heaven, so that you have to ask, "Who will ascend into heaven to get it and*

proclaim it to us so we may obey it?" Nor is it beyond the sea, so that you have to ask, "Who will cross the sea to get it and proclaim it to us so we may obey it?" No, the word is very near you; it is in your mouth and in your heart so you may obey it.

See, I set before you today life and prosperity, death and destruction. For I command you today to love the Lord your God, to walk in obedience to him, and to keep his commands, decrees and laws; then you will live and increase, and the Lord your God will bless you in the land you are entering to possess.

But if your heart turns away and you are not obedient, and if you are drawn away to bow down to other gods and worship them, I declare to you this day that you will certainly be destroyed. ... This day I call the heavens and the earth as witnesses against you that I have set before you life and death, blessings and curses. Now choose life, so that you and your children may live and that you may love the Lord your God, listen to his voice, and hold fast to him. For the Lord is your life... —Deuteronomy 30:11-19 (NIV)

BE A BLESSING AND BE BLESSED

Using our passions, talents and gifts as a lifestyle and in the way that God intended is called living and fulfilling our life's calling. Through doing this, people in the world will recognise the presence of God in our lives. This is really the crux of our purpose, because expressing our soul (full of God) using our gifts and talents, will cause people to experience the love, peace, hope, and goodness that comes with

God's presence, and our lives will be the conduit of how people will come to know and experience God in *this* life.

A UNIQUE PATH

It is also worth noting that God has an unique purpose for each of us, and thus how we will express God in our life's purpose will not necessarily be the same as the next person and that is okay because that's how God designed and created us. We all have our own idiosyncrasies that God will use to enable us to touch the lives of certain people with whom we're destined to connect. God has created us to be the representative of Him so that through our lives they'll come to know Him. We don't have to connect with the whole world, only those whom God has predestined, but we must show love to the whole world.

DISPELLING THE MYTH

Living for God is often misconstrued as living within the confines of a rigid religious system in order to gain God's approval and avoid eternal damnation. This is far from the truth because truly living for God is simply living our everyday life experiences in relationship and fellowship with Him. We incorporate His principles into our way of doing things in life, and gradually over time we morph out away from our old way of doing things into living life according to God's principles. It is this organic lifestyle change that will set us apart from people of the world, who do things their own way in ignorance to God. Our purpose is to go out into the world and be God's ambassador. When people see us living an authentically happy life and feel God's presence through our interaction with them, their lives will be touched by Him, and they'll always remember that.

I once read a quote by Maya Angelou *'People may forget what you said but they will never forget how you made them feel'*. When we use our God-given talents to positively touch people's lives, and encourage them with the hope and love that they may be needing, they are receptive to hearing more about the message of love that has already deeply resonated within them. This is how we spread and share the goodness of God with the world. Everyone has the capacity to spread God's love and presence through their every day life, from recording artists to doctors. And when we re-establish our relationship with God, we too can fulfil our destiny and positively affect people in the world in a way that only we can.

. . .

CHAPTER THIRTEEN

YOUR CALLING & PURPOSE

"That thing, that feels as natural and liberating as breathing, that makes your soul come alive... Do that!"

KNOWING OUR CALLING

Our calling otherwise known as our purpose is the work that God has created for us to do during our life on earth. Knowing our purpose has been one of life's age-old mysteries. At some point we all question the point of our lives and why we're here. Some people connect with their calling very early in life. However for the most part, we discover our calling when we begin soul-searching and investing deeply in our relationship with God. I've found that often purpose is borne out of crises where the only thing we can depend on is our faith in God, and it develops from there.

FAITHFULNESS TO GOD

Wherever our destiny in God leads us, and regardless of the level of affluence we may reach, it is fundamentally important that we absolutely maintain our faithfulness to God in all circumstances. It is through that relationship that our hearts and minds become infused with His Word and love. In this way we maintain our lives as a platform that God can continue to express Himself through in different situations, so that other people can come to experience His love and presence.

REMAINING FOCUSSED

Throughout whatever situations we may face in life, it is very important that we remain grounded in God and His purposes to avoid getting caught up in the pleasures of this world, because if we lose focus we can forfeit our relationship with God just as King Solomon did. He was the wisest King that ever lived. God gave him clear instructions for righteous living, and gave him the perfect example of a godly man in his father, King David. Yet despite all this King Solomon fully immersed himself in the pleasures of this world without any balance or boundaries. By his own account denied himself nothing that his eyes desired and refused his heart no pleasure (Ecclesiastes 2:10). This took a significant toll on his relationship with God.

We learn in 1 Kings 11 of God warning Solomon against marrying a certain culture of women whom God forbad; God knew that they would turn Solomon's heart from serving Him and upholding godly principles. King Solomon didn't listen, he married women against God's Word. After a time, just as God foreknew, Solomon's wives turned his heart to pursue false gods, and after a while his heart was no longer fully devoted to the One True God. God called Solomon's stray evil. Despite all God's warnings Solomon failed to remain faithful to God. The consequences were dire. God took ten of the twelve tribes of Israel from under Solomon's rule and lineage. This this led to the split of the Kingdom of Israel, resulting in separate states Israel and Judah. What we can learn from this is that no matter how alluring and tempting things may look, nothing good comes from disobeying God.

Further, there is an interesting cycle of the obedience and subsequent disobedience of the Children of Israel illustrated in the bible; God faithfully guided and invested in them and thus blessed them greatly as they lived in obedience to Him. However after a while they began to integrate with the people of the world. They adopted as their own the world's customs and gods and forsook the One True God, just as King Solomon did. This upset God and as a result He gave them over to be ruled by their enemies, which resulted in them living a life of great oppression, pain and difficulty. They were so badly oppressed by their enemies that it drove them back to God in repentance. Then when they repented and turned from their evil ways and back to serving God, He blessed them greatly. However, this cycle has repeated itself throughout the generations of life. This serves as a clear warning to us that the focus of our hearts and minds must faithfully remain aligned with God and His principles for living.

As we go forward with our daily lives we have to be conscious and consistent about developing our relationship with God as our priority; To love Him with all of our heart, all our soul and all our mind. By living in this way and incorporating God's principles as our lifestyle, we consistently walk the path of our destiny and fulfil our life's purpose. It is the most awesome experience to live life every day in a profoundly intimate relationship with our Creator as our guide and protector.

As previously seen, the very first step in this incredible life journey of developing a relationship with God is by us making a decision that we actually want to re-establish our relationship with God, and live the life that God has created for us. We decide that we want to do our best to commit to that relationship with God and incorporate His principles into our lives. When we decide to do this, God gives us His Holy Spirit to live in our bodies to empower us with all we need to help and direct us along our life path. This decision is what is known by saying the salvation prayer, as below:

SALVATION PRAYER

> *"Father, I know that I have broken your laws and my sins have separated me from you. I am truly sorry, and now I want to turn away from my past sinful life toward you. Please forgive me, and help me avoid sinning again. I believe that your son, Jesus Christ died for my sins, was resurrected from the dead, is alive, and hears my prayer. I invite Jesus to become the Lord of my life, to rule and reign in my heart from this day forward. Please send your Holy Spirit to help me obey You, and to do Your will for the rest of my life. In Jesus' name I pray, Amen."*

• • •

CHAPTER FOURTEEN

SALUTATION

As this book draws to an end, I pray that you will come to know God so deeply and develop an amazing relationship with Him. If you do this and remain committed to Him, your faith will be strong and you will achieve the great purposes that God has prepared for your destiny.

Remember there is no hurry and there are no shortcuts to fulfilling purpose. It's a daily process and a lifestyle of living in a deep and conscious relationship with God. Don't be hard on yourself. You will make mistakes. Though a righteous man may fall seven times, he still gets up! Always get back up. God is a loving God and is rooting to see you flourish and function in your purpose. God's grace and love are sufficient to cover you for where you may miss the mark.

Like a seed buried in the darkness, or the larva that will eventually become a butterfly, your whole destiny is laying await within you. If you water the seed of your destiny with the Word of God, and maintain a close relationship with Him, you will endure the process, blossom and your life will touch the world phenomenally. Persevere and never give up. Someone's destiny is counting on you. Your destiny is important. Eternity will celebrate your purpose fulfilled. Start today.

I'm so deeply excited for you!

• • •

NOTES

Notes